Designing Monetary and Fiscal Policy in Low-Income Countries

Abebe Aemro Selassie, Benedict Clements, Shamsuddin Tareq, Jan Kees Martijn, and Gabriel Di Bella

INTERNATIONAL MONETARY FUND

Washington DC

2006

Production: IMF Multimedia Services Division
Typesetting: Choon Lee
Figures: Theodore F. Peters, Jr.

Cataloging-in-Publication Data

Designing monetary and fiscal policy in low-income countries / Aemro
Selassie . . . [et al.] — Washington, D.C. : International Monetary Fund,
2006.
        p. cm. — (Occasional paper ; 250)

        Includes bibliographical references.
        ISBN 1-58906-496-8

        1. Monetary policy — Developing countries.   2. Fiscal policy —
Developing countries.   3. Poverty Reduction and Growth Facility
(International Monetary Fund)   4. Inflation — Developing countries.
I. Abebe Aemro Selassie.   II. Series : Occasional paper (International
Monetary Fund) ; no. 250
HG1496.D37 2006

Price: US$28.00
(US$25.00 to full-time faculty members and
students at universities and colleges)

Please send orders to:
International Monetary Fund, Publication Services
700 19th Street, N.W., Washington, D.C. 20431, U.S.A.
Tel.: (202) 623-7430   Telefax: (202) 623-7201
E-mail: publications@imf.org
Internet: http://www.imf.org

recycled paper

Contents

Tables

Figures

The following conventions are used in this publication:

- In tables, a blank cell indicates "not applicable," ellipsis points (. . .) indicate "not available," and 0 or 0.0 indicates "zero" or "negligible." Minor discrepancies between sums of constituent figures and totals are due to rounding.

- An en dash (–) between years or months (for example, 2005–06 or January–June) indicates the years or months covered, including the beginning and ending years or months; a slash or virgule (/) between years or months (for example, 2005/06) indicates a fiscal or financial year, as does the abbreviation FY (for example, FY2006).

- "Billion" means a thousand million; "trillion" means a thousand billion.

- "Basis points" refer to hundredths of 1 percentage point (for example, 25 basis points are equivalent to $\frac{1}{4}$ of 1 percentage point).

As used in this publication, the term "country" does not in all cases refer to a territorial entity that is a state as understood by international law and practice. As used here, the term also covers some territorial entities that are not states but for which statistical data are maintained on a separate and independent basis.

Preface

In 1999, the IMF established the Poverty Reduction and Growth Facility (PRGF) to make the objectives of poverty reduction and growth more central to lending operations in its poorest member countries. Against this backdrop, in this study, the IMF staff takes a close look at the IMF's monetary and fiscal policy advice, as well as program design in the context of PRGF-supported programs. In view of the marked improvement in macroeconomic outcomes in many low-income countries in recent years, the analysis focuses, in particular, on those countries that have established a certain level of macroeconomic stability—the so-called mature stabilizers.

Designing Monetary and Fiscal Policy in Low-Income Countries was prepared by a team comprising staff members from the Policy Development and Review (PDR) and Fiscal Affairs (FAD) departments. In PDR, the team included Abebe Aemro Selassie, Jan Kees Martijn, Gabriel Di Bella, and Zaijin Zhan. In FAD, the team consisted of Michael Keen, Benedict Clements, Shamsuddin M. Tareq, Kevin Fletcher, Mario Mansour, Todd Mattina, and Alejandro Simone. Qiang Cui of FAD and Luzmaria Monasi of PDR provided valuable research assistance. Overall supervision was exercised by Mark Plant and Peter S. Heller.

This paper was originally prepared as background for the IMF Executive Board discussion of the 2005 review of PRGF program design. The views expressed are those of the authors, however, and do not necessarily reflect the views of national authorities, the IMF, or IMF Executive Directors.

Abbreviations

CPI	Consumer price index
CIT	Corporate income tax
DSA	Debt sustainability assessment
EU	European Union
FAD	Fiscal Affairs department
FDI	Foreign direct investment
HIPC	Heavily Indebted Poor Countries
IEO	Independent Evaluation Office
IFS	*International Financial Statistics*
MDG	Millennium Development Goal
NDA	Net domestic assets
NFA	Net foreign assets
NIR	Net international reserves
NPV	Net present value
PDR	Policy Development and Review Department
PRGF	Poverty Reduction and Growth Facility
PRSP	Poverty Reduction Strategy Paper
PSCG	Private sector credit growth
PEM	Public expenditure management
RMSE	Root mean squared error
VAT	Value-added tax
WEO	World Economic Outlook

I Introduction

Macroeconomic outcomes in low-income countries have improved markedly in recent years. Reflecting improvements in policy implementation, increased official financial support, and a relatively benign international environment, economic growth in the poorest countries has increased from 2½ to 3 percent in the 1980s and early 1990s to some 4 percent since the mid-1990s. These higher growth rates have been associated with lower inflation rates, healthier public finances, and higher international reserves (Table 1.1). Although these growth outturns remain short of the rates required to achieve the Millennium Development Goals (MDGs), they nonetheless represent the best performance for low-income countries since the late 1970s.

However, important questions remain regarding the appropriate focus of macroeconomic policies for the next generation of IMF-supported programs in low-income countries:

- First, the large buildup of international reserves in recent years is indicative of possible tensions between exchange rate and monetary objectives, including inflation—how much scope is there for noninflationary monetary growth? What is the appropriate target range for inflation in shock-prone low-income countries?
- Second, notwithstanding the gains in other areas, progress toward external viability—a critical objective of IMF-supported programs—has been more limited, raising questions about the appropriate focus for monetary and fiscal policies.
- Third, with macroeconomic imbalances receding, an increasing number of low-income countries face a wider range of viable policy options. Should they use any fiscal space to cut excessive tax burdens, reduce high levels of domestic debt, or raise public spending to improve the provision of public services? To what extent do risks of crowding out private investment limit the scope for domestic government borrowing?
- Fourth, with more aid and debt relief in prospect in the coming years, improving the effectiveness of

public expenditures is going to be a major challenge for low-income countries.[1] What steps do countries need to take to improve absorptive capacity?

This paper considers possible adjustments in the design of IMF-supported programs, drawing on the experience of low-income countries that have successfully addressed the most apparent domestic macroeconomic imbalances. The paper, including the discussion of stylized facts and various empirical assessments, focuses on a group of 15 mature stabilizers that had achieved positive output growth at the start of their PRGF arrangements and in which inflation and the domestic government deficit had been brought under control (Box 1.1). An additional 5 or 6 other countries could have made this group, but the final sample was chosen with broad geographical representation in mind (Box 1.2) and limited to 15 to keep the analysis tractable. Importantly, the criteria used here do not include measures of external viability, which remains a serious concern in most of the countries in the sample.

Although the focus of this paper is on mature stabilizers, the paper also addresses some issues that are of relevance to other PRGF-supported programs. For example, both mature stabilizers and other countries with PRGF-supported programs face the challenge of increasing their capacity to absorb foreign aid and improving the efficiency of public spending. As such, some of the analysis is applicable to low-income countries more generally.

Section II presents the stylized facts of program design in the 15 mature stabilizers during 2000–03. Against this backdrop, Sections III and IV take up monetary and fiscal issues, respectively. Section V concludes.

---

[1]The implications of the recent Multilateral Debt Relief Initiative, in particular for the countries that have been part of the enhanced Heavily Indebted Poor Countries (HIPC) Initiative are not considered in this paper.

Table 1.1. Economic and Social Indicators in PRGF-Eligible and Other Developing Countries
(In percent a year, unless indicated otherwise)

	PRGF-Eligible Countries				Mature Stabilizers			
	1985–89	1990–94	1995–99	2000–04	1980–89	1990–94	1995–99	2000–04
Real GDP growth								
Median	3.36	2.51	4.19	4.52	2.89	1.27	4.85	4.92
Mean	3.54	−0.03	3.73	4.43	2.96	−1.28	5.44	4.99
Real GDP per capita growth								
Median	0.86	−0.85	1.87	1.79	0.78	−1.24	2.38	2.08
Mean	1.01	−2.31	1.40	2.13	0.72	−2.84	2.94	2.74
Inflation								
Median	8.87	17.94	8.30	4.60	5.29	21.76	15.56	4.99
Mean	127.57	355.40	26.53	10.36	22.16	108.15	18.44	5.47
Gross national saving (percent of GDP)								
Median	11.46	10.25	12.53	13.72	12.05	10.35	11.80	14.93
Mean	11.79	11.88	11.78	13.47	12.01	9.00	13.17	16.05
Gross fixed capital formation (percent of GDP)								
Median	16.49	18.18	18.41	19.58	16.47	19.08	19.99	21.90
Mean	28.75	22.87	20.68	20.28	21.15	19.80	21.00	22.78
Central government balance (percent of GDP)								
Median	−5.23	−5.69	−3.67	−3.96	−4.19	−5.57	−2.67	−4.62
Mean	−6.40	−7.09	−4.67	−4.54	−6.46	−6.24	−3.83	−4.51
Export volume growth								
Median	1.87	6.75	7.18	6.02	1.94	5.15	10.84	7.23
Mean	8.22	10.65	6.72	8.44	5.53	7.76	9.90	8.96
Debt-service ratio (actual percent of GDP)								
Median	14.62	14.92	15.30	14.73	14.29	23.59	17.89	15.12
Mean	17.21	26.66	21.45	16.46	16.82	25.61	25.78	14.28
External debt (face value, percent of GDP)								
Median	57.39	76.10	81.49	78.85	40.11	61.83	74.98	69.29
Mean	87.95	116.19	116.03	102.24	67.64	109.35	86.97	73.33
Gross reserves (months of imports)								
Median	1.96	2.33	3.73	4.22	1.12	3.80	5.00	6.40
Mean	4.07	4.21	5.22	6.00	3.15	4.31	6.29	7.61
Population growth								
Median	2.90	2.67	2.48	2.32	2.96	2.63	2.57	2.10
Mean	2.84	2.20	2.30	2.10	2.55	1.74	2.28	2.02
Life expectancy (years at birth)								
Median	51.12	51.92	52.31	52.58	52.26	52.86	53.36	55.06
Mean	53.50	54.31	54.53	54.11	55.45	55.61	55.72	55.41
Infant mortality (per thousand, under age 5)								
Median	...	148.00	140.00	134.50	...	148.00	143.00	137.00
Mean	...	149.60	141.14	130.72	...	138.27	130.40	118.00
Literacy (percent of population age 15+)								
Median	...	58.15	62.89	68.04	...	55.98	62.89	67.96
Mean	...	53.84	57.82	62.36	...	53.26	57.76	62.00

Sources: IMF, *World Economic Outlook*; IMF, *International Financial Statistics*; World Bank, *World Development Indicators*; and IMF staff estimates.

Box 1.1. The PRGF

In September 1999, the IMF established the PRGF to make the objectives of poverty reduction and growth more central to lending operations in its poorest member countries. PRGF-supported programs are framed around comprehensive, country-owned Poverty Reduction Strategy Papers (PRSPs) prepared by governments with the active participation of civil society and other development partners. As of September 2005, 78 low-income countries were eligible for PRGF assistance, of which 31 had a PRGF arrangement. Loans under the PRGF carry an annual interest rate of 0.5 percent and are repaid over a 10-year period.

Key Features

Experience with the PRGF highlights a number of distinctive features:

- *Broad participation and greater ownership*—the main features of PRGF-supported programs are to be drawn from the country's PRSPs. This ensures that civil society and development partners are involved in the design of the program and that country authorities are clear leaders of the process.
- *Embedding the PRGF in the overall strategy for growth and poverty reduction*—key policy measures and structural reforms supported under the program reflect each country's poverty reduction and growth priorities.
- *Budgets that are more pro-poor and pro-growth*—programs supported under the PRGF are expected to increase poverty-reducing spending, improve the efficiency and targeting of such spending, and include tax reforms that simultaneously enhance efficiency and equity, thereby generating more resources for poverty reduction strategy.
- *Ensuring appropriate flexibility in fiscal targets*—fiscal targets in PRGF-supported programs should respond flexibly to changes in country circumstances and pro-poor policy priorities while ensuring that the strategy can be financed in a sustainable, noninflationary manner.
- *More selective conditionality*—conditionality in PRGF-supported programs should be more selective and focus on a few measures that are critical to the success of the program.
- *Emphasis on measures to improve public resource management and accountability*—PRGF-supported programs focus on strengthening governance to assist countries' efforts to design targeted and well-prioritized spending. Measures to improve public resource management, transparency, and accountability are of particular importance.
- *Social impact analysis of major macroeconomic adjustment and structural reforms*—PRGF-supported programs also give more attention to the poverty and social impact of key macroeconomic policy measures.

IMF–World Bank Cooperation

PRGF-supported programs are designed to cover only areas within the primary responsibility of the IMF, unless a particular measure is judged to have a direct, critical macroeconomic impact. Areas typically covered by the IMF include advising on prudent macroeconomic policies and related structural reforms such as exchange rate and tax policy, fiscal management, budget execution, fiscal transparency, and tax and customs administration.

When appropriate, the IMF draws on World Bank expertise in designing PRGF-supported programs, and the staffs of the IMF and Bank cooperate closely on program conditionality.

Box 1.2. Why the "Mature Stabilizer" Moniker?

There is no accepted definition of a mature stabilizer. Previous IMF documents have identified such a country as one where "political and economic institutions are in place and macroeconomic stability is reasonably well established." The criteria developed in this paper are meant to capture those low-income countries that—after a period of protracted macroeconomic instability, manifested among other things in high levels of inflation (see the figure)—have achieved some degree of internal macroeconomic balance and a manageable fiscal position. Countries were selected on the basis of their performance on a number of macroeconomic criteria, including positive output growth, inflation less than 10 percent, and domestic financing of the budget deficit under 1 percent of GDP in the year before the start of the PRGF arrangement.[1]

Another label that has been used to refer to low-income countries with similar traits is "poststabilization" countries. Gupta, Verhoeven, and Tiongson (2002) and Adam and Bevan (2004) referred to similar countries as poststabilizers. The criteria used in this paper are more comprehensive. In Gupta, Verhoeven, and Tiongson (2002), poststabilization countries are defined as those with deficits under 2 percent of GDP, inflation less than 10 percent during the preprogram year and projected to remain under 10 percent during the two subsequent years, and positive growth during

the preprogram year. Adam and Bevan (2004) define a successful stabilization (and by extension, a poststabilization country) as one in which inflation declines from "high levels" to rates under 15 percent for at least two years. The World Bank (2001) suggests that a primary surplus of 3 percent of GDP would qualify a country as being in a poststabilization state.

The criteria used in this exercise do not cover external debt sustainability. Although external debt sustainability has been promoted under the PRGF and the HIPC Initiative, PRGF-supported programs have not aimed at ensuring full sustainability, as demonstrated in the 2004 review of program design.

On the basis of the criteria, 15 countries that also had PRGF-supported programs during the 2000–03 period were selected, although a few more could have qualified. The exclusion of some countries was based on the expiration of PRGF eligibility (Macedonia FYR), the start of a qualifying PRGF program period only in 2003 (Armenia and Burkina Faso), political instability (Côte d'Ivoire), and the desirability of ensuring adequate geographical representation. The countries in the sample are Albania, Azerbaijan, Bangladesh, Benin, Ethiopia, Guyana, Honduras, the Kyrgyz Republic, Madagascar, Mongolia, Mozambique, Rwanda, Senegal, Tanzania, and Uganda. Data were drawn from IMF staff reports and the World Economic Outlook (WEO) database. Given fluctuations in macroeconomic and fiscal performance, most countries did not continuously meet all three conditions. For example, of the 51 annual IMF-supported programs in these 15 countries examined between 2000 and 2003, in only 29 cases did they meet all three conditions in the preprogram year.

---

[1]This measure provides a proxy for the sustainability of domestic debt accumulation. As long as growth is positive, under most circumstances, such a low level of financing would result in no more than a moderate steady-state level of domestic debt as a share of GDP.

Median Inflation Rate in Mature Stabilizers
(In percent)

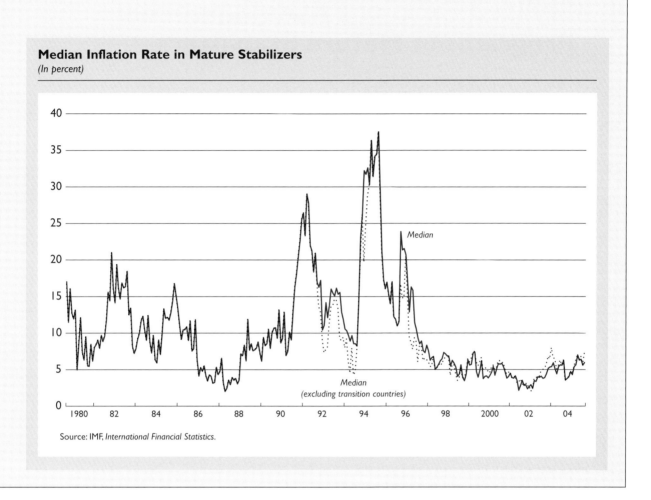

Source: IMF, *International Financial Statistics.*

II   Stylized Facts of PRGF-Supported Programs in Mature Stabilizers

PRGF-supported programs in the 15 mature stabilizers during 2000–03 have generally sought to consolidate macroeconomic stability and foster growth. By and large, growth outcomes have been in line with program targets. Reflecting favorable initial conditions, there has been limited emphasis on further disinflation. On the fiscal front, programs have sought to increase capital spending, but have not been generally successful. Developments in the external accounts have been less favorable; while external reserves have increased, current account deficits have remained too large to ensure external viability even after debt relief from the enhanced HIPC Initiative. The rest of this section discusses these stylized facts in more detail.

Growth and Inflation

After recovering in the late 1990s, economic growth in the mature stabilizers has been sustained at relatively high levels (see Table 1.1 and Figure 2.1). Growth outcomes in the 15 countries have generally been close to program projections. At inception, PRGF-supported programs in the countries typically envisaged an increase in growth from about 4½ percent in the year preceding the program to 6 percent in the third program year. But growth outcomes tended to be lower, and expectations of growth increases shifted to later years in subsequent program documents (Figure 2.2 and Box 2.1). These revised program projections (often established in the year immediately preceding the program year) are the ones with the most direct bearing on the calibration of monetary and fiscal policies. The median projection in the sampled countries one year out is for real GDP growth of 5½ percent a year—some 3 percent in per capita terms.[1]

---

[1]This growth projection of 5½ percent is surprisingly persistent. Programs in countries where growth in the year before the program was above or below 5 percent envisage growth in the program year to be 5½ percent. The outcomes closely mirror this: when growth is higher than 5 percent in the year preceding the program, actual growth turns out to be around 5¾ percent of GDP; when growth is below 5 percent in the year preceding the program, growth outcomes rise toward 5¼ percent.

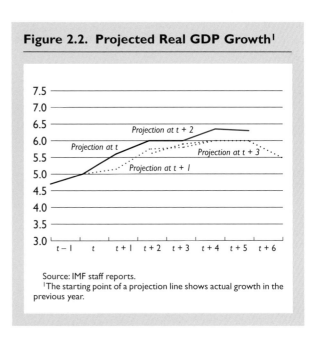

Figure 2.1. Real GDP Growth: 1980–2003[1]
(Median values in percent)

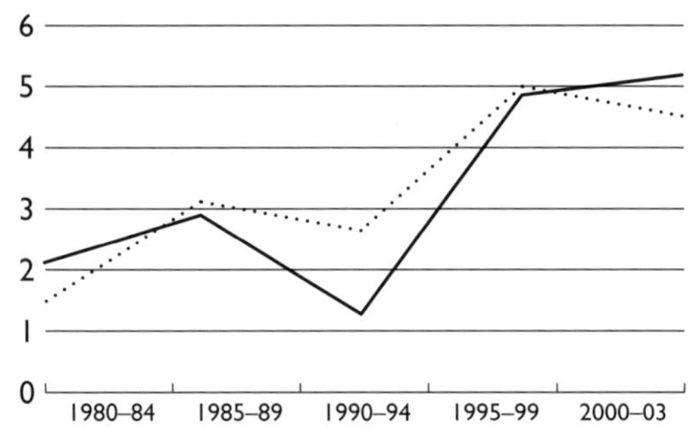

Source: IMF, *World Economic Outlook*.
[1]Dotted line excludes the three transition countries in the sample: Albania, Azerbaijan, and the Kyrgyz Republic.

Figure 2.2. Projected Real GDP Growth[1]

Source: IMF staff reports.
[1]The starting point of a projection line shows actual growth in the previous year.

Box 2.1. Targets and Projections in IMF-Supported Programs

The projections for the original program may not be the most relevant ones for the entire program period. Program projections are updated regularly—in principle at each half-yearly program review.

Macroeconomic policies and outcomes are likely affected by the IMF-supported policy programs presented in both staff reports issued during the year concerned (year t), as well as by the last one presented in the previous year ($t - 1$). The projections contained in the latter report may be the most relevant ones for shaping the budget and affecting year-end policy outcomes regarding broad money and inflation, given the time lags in the transmission of monetary policy, often estimated at about 6 to 12 months. However, the current-year projections underpin the program's quantitative conditionality regarding fiscal balances and the central bank's balance sheet, which should have an impact on policy-making during the year.

Projection horizon differs across countries and variables. Program documents generally include projections for inflation and GDP for the next two or three years, but the projection period for broad money is often shorter, and reserve money and central bank NDA and NFA projections often do not extend beyond one year (that is, $t + 1$).

Table 2.1. Inflation Targets in Original PRGF-Supported Programs[1]
(In percent)

	Projection for Year				
	$t - 1$	t	$t + 1$	$t + 2$	$t + 3$
CPI (end-year)					
Average	6.5	4.7	4.5	3.9	3.8
Median	5.8	4.8	4.0	3.8	3.9
GDP deflator					
Average	7.8	5.1	4.5	3.8	3.9
Median	7.0	4.9	4.0	3.8	4.0
No. of observations	14	14	14	14	11

Sources: IMF staff reports and World Economic Outlook database.

[1]Originating programs are those reported in the staff report requesting a new arrangement under the PRGF, and for Azerbaijan, also the 2001 program augmentation.

Outcomes were only marginally (less than ½ percentage point) lower, and this difference between projections and outcome was not statistically significant.

These growth targets and outcomes are high by historic standards, but for most countries, they fall short of the levels considered necessary to achieve the MDGs. Until the second half of the 1990s, real growth in the mature stabilizer sample was anemic, averaging 3 percent or lower. Although real GDP growth has picked up since the mid-1990s, the countries in the sample have not attained the approximately 7 percent growth rates that are considered necessary to meet the MDG target of halving poverty by 2015. Why, then, don't the authorities generally target higher growth rates? Some clearly do—for example, one-fifth (10) of the PRGF-supported program episodes under consideration target growth rates of 7 percent or more. Elsewhere, the modest growth objectives likely reflect estimates of potential growth, and the caution exhibited in program growth targets does not seem to be out of order.[2]

On the inflation front, the overall focus of PRGF-supported programs has been gradual further disinflation:

- At the inception of a new PRGF-supported program, inflation was generally projected to decline to less than 4 percent over the three-year program period from more than 6 percent in the year before the start of the program, as shown in Table 2.1.[3] The final-year projections across the programs ranged from 2 to 6 percent. Average and median projected inflation were close, reflecting the scarcity of large outliers in this sample limited to countries that already had largely disinflated. However, as with growth projections, the inflation targets that matter most for program design purposes, and around which monetary and fiscal policies are calibrated, are the ones set shortly before and during program episodes under consideration. During the arrangement period, these inflation targets tend to be adjusted upward by about 1 percentage point—to around 6 percent—to take into account somewhat higher inflation outturns (Table 2.2).[4] The magnitude of this revision is related to inflation overruns in the previous year.

---

[2]For the mature stabilizers sample, a univariate filter was used to extract the trend path for output for each country. In all cases, GDP growth in the sample in recent years has been well above the path suggested by the extracted series.

[3]The quantitative analysis in this paragraph is based on annual data for 1999–2003 for 13 of the 15 PRGF countries in the sample of stabilized economies. Benin and Senegal are not included in view of their membership in the CFA franc zone.

[4]Because the number of observations is larger closer to the target year, the panel is unbalanced and data are not fully comparable across columns. For the 29 (43) cases in which $t - 2$ ($t - 1$) data are available, the ultimate upward revision in the average inflation rate projection was from 4.1 (4.9) to 5.0 (5.3) percent, rather than to 5.9 percent.

Table 2.2. Inflation Targets in Consecutive Program Updates[1]
(In percent)

	Projection in Year				Outcome in Year	
	$t-2$	$t-1$	$t(SR1)$	$t(SR2)$	$t-1$	t
CPI (end-year)						
Average for all years	4.1	4.9	6.0	5.9	6.4	6.3
Median for all years	3.8	5.0	5.3	5.3	5.8	5.4
Median depending on actual $t-1$ inflation						
$t-1$ inflation < 5%	3.0	3.5	4.2	3.8	2.1	4.4
5% > $t-1$ inflation < 10%	3.9	5.0	6.0	6.0	6.4	5.8
$t-1$ inflation > 10%	5.0	5.5	8.5	8.5	14.4	9.6
GDP deflator						
Average for all years	4.3	5.2	6.3	6.1	6.8	6.8
Median for all years	4.0	4.8	5.2	5.1	6.5	6.3
Median depending on actual $t-1$ inflation						
$t-1$ inflation < 5%	4.0	4.0	4.2	3.6	3.1	3.9
5% > $t-1$ inflation < 10%	4.3	5.3	6.0	6.0	8.4	7.3
$t-1$ inflation > 10 %	5.6	6.7	9.2	9.2	10.6	10.6
No. of observations	29	43	54	54		

Source: IMF staff reports and World Economic Outlook database.

[1]The projections are for year t. The projections as of year $t-1$ and $t-2$ are those from the last staff report in the previous year and the year before that, respectively. The projection as of $t(SR1)$ is from the first staff report in year t, and the one at $t(SR2)$ is from the final staff report in that year. If only one staff report was issued in year t, the last two observations coincide.

- Based on this revised metric—inflation as targeted in the year before—the approximately 50 program episodes under consideration projected inflation of 5 percent, and outturns have been relatively close.[5] There are few significant deviations between targets and outcomes. In those instances when inflation was above 10 percent in the year before the program, a gradual reduction of inflation was envisaged. In the 11 such cases, the median inflation was targeted to decelerate from 14½ percent in the year preceding the program episode to 9 percent in the first program year.
- Overall, then, inflation did recede during these PRGF-supported programs, albeit somewhat less than projected. On average, consumer price index (CPI) inflation moderated from more than 9 percent in the year before the start of the program to less than 5 percent three years later—about 1 percentage point above the original program target.[6]

Fiscal Developments

PRGF-supported programs in the sampled countries have sought to keep the overall budget deficit broadly unchanged (at 4½ percent of GDP), with modest increases in spending targeted to be offset by an increase in revenues (Table 2.3).

Specifically:
- On average, public expenditure was targeted to increase by some ¾ percentage point of GDP a year, with most of the increase targeted for higher capital outlays consistent with the growth orientation of PRGF-supported programs. In general, countries with higher initial spending (in relation to GDP) targeted smaller increases (or larger declines) in expenditure (Figure 2.3).[7] Current spending and the wage bill, in contrast, were targeted to remain broadly unchanged.
- This increase in expenditures was expected to be offset by an improvement in tax revenues and

[5]Depending on data availability, the precise number of episodes varies slightly for the various statistics presented in this section.

[6]This moderation in inflation should not be attributed solely to the PRGF-supported programs. There has been a marked drop in inflation across the world. Indeed, the decline in median inflation in the sample is no larger than witnessed in other developing countries.

[7]Notable exceptions were Albania (2001, 2002), Guyana (2000), and Honduras (2001). In all three cases, the initial level of spending was much higher than the sample mean (about 26 percent of GDP).

Table 2.3. Fiscal Targets and Performance
(Unweighted averages in percent of GDP)

	Actual Level $t-1$	Targeted Change $t-1$ to t	Actual Change $t-1$ to t
Number of annual arrangements	51	51	51
Total revenue and grants	22.1	0.8	0.7
Revenue	18.0	0.5	0.5
Tax revenue	14.8	0.6	0.6
Nontax revenue	3.3	−0.1	−0.1
Grants	4.0	0.3	0.2
Total expenditure and net lending[1]	26.2	0.8	0.4
Current expenditure	17.6	0.1	0.5
Wages and salaries	5.9	0.1	0.2
Interest	2.2	−0.1	−0.2
Capital expenditure and net lending	8.3	0.7	0.0
Foreign-financed capital expenditure[2]	4.3	0.3	−0.2
Other fiscal transactions[3]	0.4	0.1	0.0
Overall balance (including grants)	−4.5	−0.1	0.3
Overall balance (excluding grants)	−8.6	−0.3	0.2
Financing			
External financing	4.0	−0.1	−0.3
Project loans[4]	3.1	0.2	−0.2
Domestic financing	0.6	0.2	0.0

Sources: National authorities and IMF staff estimates.

[1]Total expenditure and net lending includes spending items that are not classified as current or capital.

[2]Data on foreign-financed capital spending are not available for Bangladesh, Honduras, and Guyana.

[3]Other fiscal transactions include repayment of arrears and float.

[4]Data on project loans are not available for Bangladesh and Honduras.

Figure 2.3. Expenditure Targets in PRGF Programs, 2000–03
(In percent of GDP)

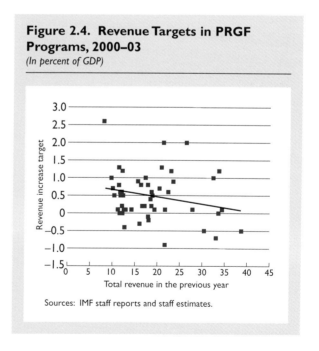

Sources: IMF staff reports and staff estimates.

Figure 2.4. Revenue Targets in PRGF Programs, 2000–03
(In percent of GDP)

Sources: IMF staff reports and staff estimates.

grants of the same order of magnitude (Figure 2.4).

- Deficits (relative to GDP) were programmed on average to be unchanged. Relatively few programs targeted a significant increase in domestic financing—even when the level of domestic debt was low—with an average increase in domestic financing 0.2 percent of GDP.
- Finally, the broad stability in the targeted fiscal balance contrasts with the lower fiscal deficit and domestic financing typically envisaged in other PRGF programs where internal macroeconomic stability remained a concern. For example, in a

sample of 18 countries with PRGF-supported programs for such countries over the same period, the overall deficit was targeted to decline by about 1½ percent of GDP.

Fiscal deficits in PRGF-supported programs have, however, been smaller than envisaged because of

Box 2.2. Social and Poverty-Reducing Spending[1]

Programs in the mature stabilizer sample have achieved significant increases in poverty-reducing spending. The average PRGF-supported program achieved an increase of about 1 percent of GDP (2¾ percent of total spending) in these outlays a year (see the figure). Average annual spending on poverty-reducing programs increased by more than 2 percent of GDP in Ethiopia, Guyana, and Mozambique, and

[1]The sample comprises 42 programs for social spending and 40 programs for poverty-reducing spending. Social spending is defined as education and health care expenditures.

by more than 1 percent of GDP in Tanzania and Uganda. Honduras was the only country in the sample where the ratio decreased; there was practically no increase in Benin and Madagascar. Over the 1999–2002 period, these outlays in the sampled countries rose by more than 3 percent of GDP. Social spending (outlays on education and health care) has also risen. The average social spending to GDP ratio increased in all countries in the sample except Azerbaijan and the Kyrgyz Republic. Thus, the mature stabilizers have achieved a modicum of success in making their budgets more pro-poor, despite difficulties in raising total government spending to the extent programmed. Although it is possible that changes in classification may account for part of these increases, they have nonetheless been accompanied by improvements in social indicators for which data are available (see the table).

Average Annual Increase in Social and Poverty-Reducing Spending Realized in Mature Stabilizers[1]

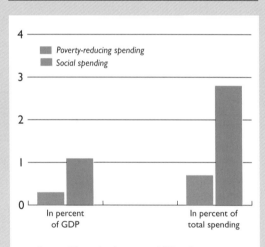

Sources: National authorities; and IMF staff estimates.
[1]In many countries, budgetary data do not cover all public spending in social and poverty-reducing sectors. Nonpublic spending in these sectors could also be significant in some countries.

Average Annual Improvement in Selected Social Indicators[1]
(Percent change, positive indicating improvement)

	Average Annual Improvement	Countries in Sample
Infant mortality rate	1.8	15
Under-five mortality rate	1.9	15
Births attended by skilled staff	−0.4	9
Primary school enrollment rate	2.2	14
Female primary school enrollment rate	2.9	14

Source: World Bank, World Development Indicators database.
[1]Average annual improvement refers to the annual change between 1999 and the latest available year, usually 2001. Positive growth rates correspond to improved outcomes.

shortfalls in capital spending. The mature stabilizers did not raise capital outlays as a share of GDP, mainly because of shortfalls in foreign project implementation. These shortfalls were partially offset by current spending that was higher than programmed, including for wages. The composition of spending has also shifted toward social and poverty-reducing spending as sought under the Poverty Reduction Strategy Paper (PRSP) approach (see Box 2.2). Revenue collection

as a share of GDP was broadly in line with program projections. As a result, the fiscal deficit was about ½ percent of GDP smaller than envisaged. These averages mask a great deal of variation in targets. For instance, several PRGF-supported programs have accommodated large increases in the fiscal deficit to accommodate higher external financing—for example, Guyana (2000), Mozambique (2000), Rwanda (2000), and Tanzania (2002).

Figure 2.5. External Development Indicators in the Mature Stabilizers

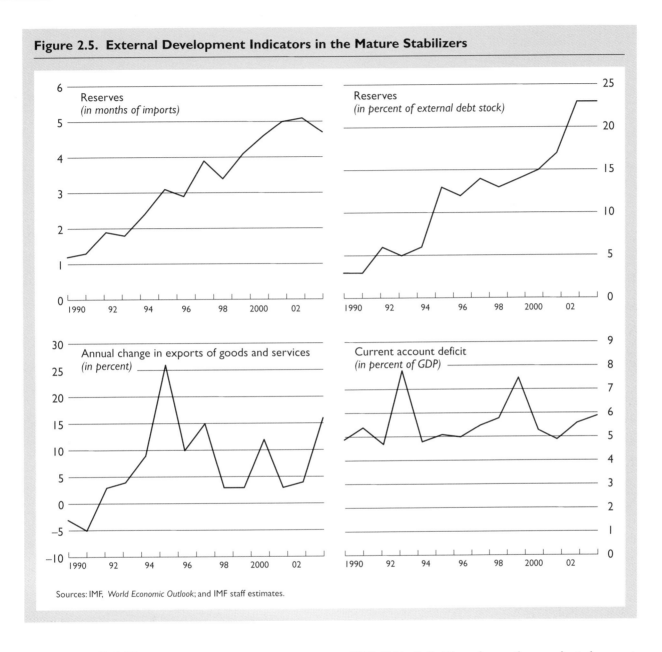

Sources: IMF, *World Economic Outlook*; and IMF staff estimates.

External Viability

Progress toward external viability among the mature stabilizers has been limited. On the positive front, international reserves have increased significantly in the 15 countries, from less than three months to about five months of import cover since the mid-1990s, increasing the scope for absorbing the impact of shocks (Figure 2.5, top left panel). This improvement in part reflected an increase in aid inflows (including debt relief) as well as a recovery in export growth (Figure 2.5, lower left panel). Current account deficits have been lowered relative to program targets (by about 1¼ percentage points of

GDP, Table 2.4). These lower-than-projected current account deficits and close adherence to fiscal deficit targets imply a lower-than-projected investment-savings imbalance by the private sector.[8] Nonetheless, these current account deficits (net of foreign direct investment [FDI]) have been too high to stabilize the stock of net present value (NPV) of debt—including after HIPC Initiative debt relief (Figure 2.6). In particular:

_____

[8]Possibly reflecting the pickup in growth since the mid-1990s, private saving has increased steadily in the mature-stabilizers (Table 1.1).

Table 2.4. External Targets versus Outcomes in the Mature Stabilizer Sample

	Program	Actual	Difference
Current account balance (percent of GDP)	−6.9	−5.7	−1.2
Reserves (months of imports)	4.2	4.5	−0.3

Sources: IMF, staff reports and World Economic Outlook database.

Figure 2.6. Actual and Debt-Stabilizing Current Account Balances[1]

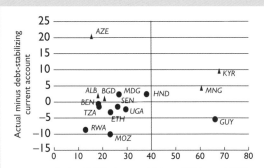

Ratio of NPV of external debt to GDP at end-2003 (including completion point debt relief for HIPCs)

Source: IMF, World Economic Outlook database.
[1]Debt figures include actual or expected completion point debt relief for HIPCs. Triangles show the values for non-HIPCs.
Note: Country abbreviations used are ISO codes. ALB=Albania; AZE=Azerbaijan; BEN=Benin; BGD=Bangladesh; ETH=Ethiopia; GUY=Guyana; HND=Honduras; KYR=Kyrgyz Rep.; MDG=Madagascar; MNG=Mongolia; MOZ=Mozambique; RWA=Rwanda; SEN=Senegal; TZA=Tanzania; UGA=Uganda.

- In eight countries (those below the line at zero), the current account deficits during 2000–03 were too high to stabilize the external debt stock. All of these countries are HIPCs. And while they are accumulating debt from moderate levels reflecting the debt relief that has been provided to them,[9] these findings nonetheless suggest that external debt buildup will resume anew unless steps are taken to curb borrowing, move to grant financing, or both.[10]

- The other seven countries (including Honduras, which benefited from HIPC debt relief) have sustained current account deficits that would allow them to stabilize or even reduce their external debt stocks—though from a very high level in the case of Mongolia and the Kyrgyz Republic.

External viability has not received adequate attention in PRGF program design, although the findings are somewhat more encouraging for this sample group than for the broader sample of PRGF countries (IMF, 2004c). One reason is that conditionality in IMF-supported programs seldom limited either the overall fiscal balance or external borrowing on concessional terms. Of the 38 PRGF arrangements in place at end-March 2003, only 12 arrangements had conditionality to limit either the overall or primary fiscal balance and no arrangement had direct limits on concessional borrowing. Of course, poor use of concessional resources is one reason that low-income countries have built up unsustainable debt burdens in the past.

Figure 2.7. Ratio of Private Investment to GDP[1]
(Median values in percent)

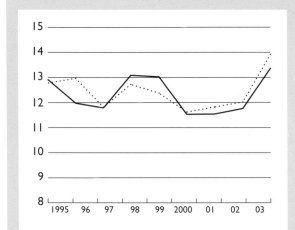

Source: IMF, World Economic Outlook database.
[1]Dotted line excludes the three transition countries in the samples: Albania, Azerbaijan, and the Kyrgyz Republic.

---

[9]Guyana stands out as a country with a rather high post-HIPC debt ratio relative to GDP, and it is set to rapidly accumulate new external debt. Its debt is more modest relative to exports (a measure of debt-servicing capacity) and is substantially below the related HIPC threshold, reflecting the high share of exports in GDP.

[10]The vertical line in Figure 2.6, at 40 percent NPV of external debt to GDP, marks the threshold where the risk of debt distress increases for countries with a medium rating for the quality of their policies and institutions by the World Bank's Country Policy and Institutional Assessment (see IMF, 2005d). All of the countries in the sample have a medium or better rating.

More recently, the incorporation of debt sustainability assessments (DSAs) in the IMF's operational work on low-income countries should allow PRGF-supported programs to focus more explicitly on debt sustainability considerations. This will not fully resolve the tension between increasing poverty-reducing expenditures and making progress toward external viability, but it will help clarify the longer-term implications of near-term fiscal decisions (IMF, 2004a, 2004b, 2005d). Importantly, these assessments, which look at the issue of debt sustainability from many angles, will help signal to donors the need for grant financing when there is a higher likelihood of debt distress.

In sum, the mature stabilizers have done relatively well, with markedly higher growth, lower inflation, and higher international reserves, but continuing concerns about external viability. An important question, however, is whether the recent pickup in growth can be sustained or, better still, improved upon. Since 1995, private investment, arguably the most telling predictor of future growth performance, has edged up in the countries in the sample (see Figure 2.7). With the exception of Tanzania and Uganda, where it has been broadly flat, private investment in 2000–03 was marginally higher than in the late 1990s. But this improvement is modest and leaves investment ratios low relative to other regions.

III Monetary Policy Issues in PRGF-Supported Programs

As noted above, maintaining inflation in the low single digits is an important feature of PRGF-supported programs in the mature stabilizers. In general, programs sought to keep inflation in the 4–6 percent range. The next two parts of this section consider the appropriateness of these targets and the monetary policy framework in which these targets have been pursued. A third part considers the nexus between private sector credit growth, fiscal policy, and economic activity.

Inflation and Economic Growth

The 15 countries considered in this review have kept inflation at relatively low levels for a sustained period, but the benefits of this achievement have been questioned. Critics have argued that such inflation has required high real interest rates and constrained potential seigniorage income. Although unanimity exists in the economic literature on the costs of very high inflation, consensus is lacking on the appropriate inflation range for low-income countries.[1] More generally, the scope for monetary policy to impede growth far exceeds its ability to create it: high inflation—above, for example, 40 percent—is certainly inimical to growth, but keeping inflation low will not by itself induce a growth boom. Against this backdrop, this section considers the appropriate inflation range for low-income countries.

High inflation is harmful to economic growth, but the gains from continued moderate inflation on growth are ambiguous, reflecting the multitude of transmission channels.[2] On the one hand, as inflation accelerates, a negative effect on growth is likely, given the associated increase in inflation uncertainty, which clouds price signals and limits both the quantity and quality of investments. On the other hand, some inflation could enhance real wage flexibility, or help avoid liquidity trap problems. In case of price stickiness, a low inflation target could render an economy vulnerable to prolonged downturns if adverse supply shocks were to occur (see below). Empirical analysis aimed at untangling these effects is hindered by the possibility of reverse causality—from growth to inflation and the endogeneity of both variables. For example, high inflation may signal poor institutions and policies more generally and be associated with lower growth as a result.[3]

Notwithstanding this complexity, considerable empirical support exists for policies that aim at keeping inflation between, say, 5 and 10 percent. The existence of a negative relationship between inflation and growth at higher rates of inflation is empirically well supported. By contrast, identifying the growth effects of moving from, say, 20 percent inflation to 5 percent has been challenging. According to Bruno and Easterly (1998), significant adverse growth effects can be found only for generally short-lived periods of high inflation, after which growth tends to return to its long-run path—classic money neutrality. However, several other studies indicate this may understate the adverse growth effects of moderate inflation:

- Examinations of prolonged episodes of accelerated growth show that the onset of such periods is typically associated with lower inflation and that, moreover, the upfront improvement in macroeconomic

---

[1]Given the close association between the level and the variability of inflation, their respective effects cannot easily be disentangled empirically. The positive relation also implies that the distinction may be of little relevance for policy purposes.

[2]According to empirical work undertaken in the recent papers on the design of IMF-supported programs, there is no evidence that the monetary stance (measured by velocity) was set excessively tight in IMF-supported programs, leading to lower output growth (IMF, 2004f, Section III.B). Similarly, the Independent Evaluation Office (IEO) found no evidence suggesting "an excessive deflationary bias with respect to inflation targets" (IEO, 2004). For an overview of this and other effects of inflation on growth, see Temple (2000).

[3]Easterly and Levine (2003) find no significant impact of macroeconomic policies (averaged over four decades) on the level of economic development after controlling for the impact of institutions, and Easterly (2004) conjectures that any impact of macroeconomic policies found in growth regressions may occur through its performance as a proxy for institutional quality. This view, however, contrasts with a range of evidence (see below) that is suggestive of an independent role of macroeconomic stabilization. It is likely that both macroeconomic stabilization and institutional improvements are important in triggering and sustaining higher rates of economic growth.

Table 3.1. Empirical Studies on Kinks in the Relationship between Inflation and Growth

	Inflation Threshold (percent)	Growth Effect of Higher Inflation Below the Threshold	Countries	Period	Inflation Measure	Remarks
Fischer (1993)	15	Negative	80	1960–89	CPI	
Barro (1996)	10–20	Not significant	117	1960–90	10-year average CPI	
Sarel (1996)	8	Positive	87	1970–90	5-year average CPI	
Bruno and Easterly (1998)	40	Not significant	97	1961–92	CPI	
Ghosh and Phillips (1998)	>5	Positive	145	1960–96	Average annual CPI	
Kochhar and Coorey (1999)	5	Positive	84 (low- and middle-income countries only)	1981–95	Average annual CPI	
Khan and Senhadji (2001)	11–12 (for developing countries only)	Not significant	140	1960–98	5-year average CPI	1–3 percent threshold for industrial countries. Controlled for investment and unemployment.
Burdekin and others (2000)	3 (for developing countries only)	Positive	51	1967–92		8 percent threshold for industrial countries.
Gylfason and Herbertsson (2001)	10–20	Positive	170	1960–92	5-year average GDP deflator	

indicators is more generalized for longer episodes of growth acceleration than for shorter ones.[4]

- Quantifying the association between inflation and growth requires careful attention to the nonlinearities in the relationship between inflation and growth. This relationship appears to be convex: a given increase in inflation is associated with a larger negative growth effect, the lower the initial rate of inflation. But at low rates, higher inflation may have no effect on growth or its effect may even be positive. Since the work of Fischer (1993), several authors have tried to identify and locate such a "kink" in the relationship between inflation and economic growth associated with a maximum growth rate. Empirical studies using panels of countries have located this kink in the inflation-growth nexus at a level of inflation somewhere between 3 percent and 40 percent, with a cluster suggesting a level in the 5–10 percent range (see Table 3.1). Moreover, a positive growth effect of higher inflation was found at relatively low levels of inflation, suggesting that higher-than-single-digit inflation would not promote growth, while entailing risks of a negative effect. Notably, however, most of these studies have not focused on the kink in low-income countries as opposed to broader country groupings, and none of the studies covers the period since 2000.

Additional considerations in favor of determined inflation control relate to policy credibility and poverty alleviation. For countries that have only recently managed to achieve single-digit inflation—which includes almost all in this sample of PRGF countries—it may be wise to anchor successful disinflation by maintaining inflation in the single-digit range. Indeed, the gains from price stabilization may be realized in full only when low inflation is institutionalized and incorporated into expectations. Another consideration is that price stability may foster poverty reduction directly, in addition to its impact through economic growth. Inflation tends to hurt the poor disproportionally, because they often hold no financial assets that provide a hedge against inflation or they are dependent on state-determined income that is not fully indexed.[5]

---

[4]World Bank and IMF (2005, Box 2.6).

[5]In cross-country panel studies, Li and Zou (2002) found a negative impact of higher inflation on income distribution, while Bulíř (2001) found evidence of such effect for a reduction in inflation to less than 40 percent. Fischer and Easterly (2001) used polling data to show that across countries the poor are more likely than the rich to report inflation as a personal problem.

Box 3.1. Seigniorage Income

Increases in reserve money beyond the amount that accommodates changes in real money demand tend to be inflationary, and the associated part of seigniorage is aptly called the inflation tax.[1] The reduction in inflation in PRGF countries has, indeed, entailed a decline in seigniorage revenue. Evidence suggests that seigniorage revenue (as measured below) is highest for inflation at 30–40 percent, far above the actual 6 percent average rate in this paper's sample of PRGF countries.[2] Seigniorage as a share of GDP can be expressed as[3]

$$s = r_{t-1}*(1 + g_r) - r_{t-1}/[(1 + g_p)*(1 + g_y)],$$

where r_{t-1} is the previous period's reserve money ratio (as a fraction of nominal GDP), and g_r, g_p, and g_y are the growth rates of the reserve money ratio, the price level, and real GDP, respectively. For a constant reserve money ratio of 11 percent (the average in the country sample) and an average real growth rate of 5 percent, the noninflationary level of seigniorage would amount to 0.5 percent of GDP. With 6 percent inflation, seigniorage would amount to 1.1 percent of GDP. The actual 1999–2003 average in the sample was somewhat higher, at 1.4 percent of GDP, owing to a trend increase in reserve money as a share of GDP.

However, the revenue benefits of accomodating higher inflation rates would be very limited. For one, the inflation tax is relatively distortionary (especially at higher rates, see above) and regressive (given the impact of inflation on poverty), implying a strong case against the use of higher inflation as a means of raising government resources. A more compelling case for relying on seignorage income could be the relative insufficiency of most low-income countries' tax systems. It is therefore possible that, on balance, a somewhat higher inflation tax would be less distortionary than the regular tax it could replace. But the revenue effect of raising inflation from 6 percent to, for example, 15 percent would be modest. With no change in the reserve money ratio, the revenue impact would be equivalent to 0.8 percent of GDP. But higher inflation would likely entail some decline in money demand and thereby in the reserve money ratio. Incorporating this effect could reduce the seigniorage bonus by half.[4] Thus the seignorage that could be generated from allowing inflation to rise to 15 percent would only be around 0.5 percent of GDP, and it is highly questionable whether this gain would be worth the adverse effect that higher inflation tends to have on the poor.

---

[1]Seigniorage revenue typically takes the form of a profit transfer from the central bank to the government. In cases where the central bank lends to the government at below-market interest rates, reducing the bank's profits, the transfer may appear as lower interest payments.

[2]Phillips (1999).

[3]The formula does not take into account the remuneration of commercial bank reserves within reserve money. However, in the country sample, currency in circulation accounts for more than 60 percent of reserve money, on average, and remuneration is limited.

[4]During 1994–2003, for disinflating nontransition PRGF-supported programs, a 1 percentage point increase in inflation was associated with a rise in velocity (and thereby in the reciprocal of the reserve money ratio) by about 0.4 percent (IMF, 2004d, Box 5).

Some observers have argued that tight monetary policies have adversely affected poverty alleviation by constraining government spending. The main channel through which monetary policy can reduce available fiscal resources is by lowering seigniorage—that is, government revenue from an increase in reserve money (see Box 3.1).[6] However, the revenue effect of raising inflation from 6 percent to, for example, 15 percent would be modest because seigniorage revenue would be raised by less than 0.4 percentage point of GDP.

One strong argument in support of higher inflation targets for developing countries is the need to accommodate exogenous shocks. Developing countries are more prone to supply shocks, such as adverse weather conditions, and sharp changes in the terms of trade. Moreover, the aggregate impact of such shocks may be more pronounced as a result of the limited diversification of production and consumption and the prevalence of de facto trade barriers (including, for example, lack of transportation and integrated distribution networks). Adverse supply shocks would tend to push up prices while limiting economic growth. In the presence of downward nominal rigidities, inflation targets that do not accommodate the supply shocks could serve to amplify their adverse growth effects. This consideration argues for inflation targets that accommodate the first-round effect of supply shocks (unless the shock is expected to be undone within a few months—that is, before monetary policy is effectively transmitted).

Cross-country evidence demonstrates the higher vulnerability of PRGF countries to external shocks.

---

[6]In addition, tight monetary policy could raise real interest rates on government debt, lowering the room for spending. This channel is not considered in this paper. These effects of monetary policy on the government's intertemporal budget constraint should be distinguished from controls over government borrowing, which affect the distribution over time of primary government spending.

The year-on-year volatility of the terms of trade and export volumes (which may to a large extent be considered exogenous) and of real GDP growth (which also incorporates the policy response) is relatively large in PRGF countries, and in low-income countries more generally, in comparison with advanced and transition economies.[7]

Program design should address such volatility. In particular, programs can accommodate adverse supply shocks (within limits) while avoiding second-round effects, thus stabilizing inflation expectations.

- Programs could be based on a target range for inflation around the operational (core) target, especially in countries where substantial exogenous shocks have occurred. For example, as illustrated in Figure 3.1, a band of 2 percentage points above and below the central target would capture more than 60 percent of realizations. Such change would not directly alter the monetary targets or the associated conditionality, but would formalize the inflation tolerance that is, in practice, often already exhibited in programs. The change may also help improve policy credibility by reducing the likelihood that inflation targets are missed. One of the risks associated with this approach is that, in practice, policies may simply be redirected toward the higher end of the inflation range, in which case the result would be an unwarranted policy relaxation with no increase in flexibility.[8]

- In some cases, consideration could be given to focusing on measures of core inflation rather than the overall CPI in PRGF-supported programs.[9] The monetary targets would continue to be based on nominal income and incorporate the first-round effects, while preventing second-round effects that would lift core inflation.

On balance, these considerations support the use of single-digit inflation targets. Preserving the inflation gains already achieved by the countries in this sample is of vital importance. There is a need to further ingrain and institutionalize this achievement, enhancing the credibility, and thus the desirability, of the low-inflation strategy. However, pushing inflation too low—say, below 5 percent—may entail

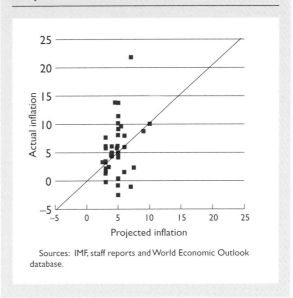

Figure 3.1. Inflation: One-Year-Ahead Projections and Outcomes

Sources: IMF, staff reports and World Economic Outlook database.

a loss of output and seigniorage revenue, suggesting a need for caution in setting very low inflation targets in low-income countries. These countries tend to be subject to larger output volatility and more pronounced price shocks, and program design should take these economic attributes properly into account. In particular, inflation targets should be set so as to help avoid risks of an unintended contractionary policy stance.

Financial Programming

This part of the section considers the effectiveness of reserve money targets and program conditionality as an anchor for monetary policy. There are several reasons for this assessment at this juncture. For one, as demonstrated in the 2004 review of the design of IMF-supported programs (IMF, 2004d), the commonly applied net domestic assets (NDA)–net international reserves (NIR) framework is not well suited for controlling inflation, which generally requires a more explicit monetary anchor. These papers also underscore the need to offset the monetary impact of donor support if inflation targets are to be met. Second, the large buildup of international reserves—beyond program targets—in the mature stabilizers could be indicative of the policy challenges related to reconciling exchange rate and monetary objectives.

Reserve money serves as an operational target for the 13 sampled countries that do not have a formal

---

[7]The 1995–2003 average standard deviation of the annual growth rates of export volumes, the terms of trade, and real GDP deviated significantly (at a 1 percent level for the first two variables and at a 5 percent level for the latter) between low-income countries and advanced economies, and for the terms of trade also relative to transition economies (at a 10 percent level).

[8]Another risk is that target bands may be less effective at helping shape expectations.

[9]However, in low-income countries, volatile food prices often constitute a large share of the overall CPI, severely limiting the operational relevance of measures of core inflation.

Box 3.2. Monetary Programming in IMF Program Design

Monetary policy targets for low-income countries are generally derived through financial programming. Financial programming involves the use of balance sheet relationships and a few simple behavioral relationships. It helps ensure the consistency of the design of monetary policy with (1) goals or assumptions regarding real GDP growth and inflation; (2) projected domestic financing of the budget and provision of sufficient credit to the private sector; and (3) the balance of payments (BoP) outlook as reflected in the net accumulation of foreign assets by commercial banks and the monetary authorities. Within financial programming, the exercise that directly relates to the central bank's monetary program is also referred to as reserve money programming.[1]

The level of broad money (M) that would be consistent with the program targets for inflation (P, the GDP deflator) and real income (Y) is derived using the identity

$$M*V = P*Y, \tag{1}$$

where V is the velocity of circulation. In terms of growth rates:

$$(1 + g_M) = (1 + g_P)*(1 + g_Y)*[(1 + 1/(1 + g_V)]. \tag{2}$$

Velocity depends on such factors as interest rates and changes in inflation, but it is typically—including in the mature stabilizers sample—assumed to remain constant over the program period. Provided that the assumption on velocity adequately reflects money demand, limiting the growth in money supply in line with equation (2) should help realize the targeted rate of inflation.

The increase in reserve money (RM) that would support this broad money target is generally derived from

$$M = m*RM, \tag{3}$$

or

$$(1 + g_M) = (1 + g_m)*(1 + g_{RM}), \tag{4}$$

where m is the reserve money multiplier, which reflects the ratio of currency in circulation to bank deposits and banks' holdings of reserves at the central bank. Like velocity, the multiplier is often assumed constant over the program period.

Target values for the central bank's NDA and NFA are derived using

$$\Delta RM = \Delta NFA + \Delta NDA. \tag{5}$$

Similarly, for the banking sector (B) as a whole,

$$\Delta M = (\Delta NFAB) + (\Delta NDAB)$$
$$= (BoP) + (\Delta CG + \Delta CP + \Delta BNW), \tag{6}$$

with CG equal to net banking sector credit to the government, CP equal to net banking sector credit to the private sector, and BNW equal to net worth of the banking sector (often assumed constant over the program period). An important application of equation (6) allows verification if, given the targets and projections for the other variables, projected government borrowing is consistent with (does not crowd out) the scope for lending to the private sector, which, in turn, is important to sustaining private sector growth.

---

[1]For a more general overview, see IMF (2004f, Appendix I).

---

exchange rate peg (Box 3.2).[10] The increase in reserve money projected to be in line with the inflation objective in turn provides the basis for the standard program ceiling on central bank NDA and the floor on central bank NIR or net foreign assets (NFA).[11] Importantly, this framework does not constrain reserve money growth—that is, it does not provide a monetary anchor. In particular, the existence of a floor on central bank NFA provides scope for larger reserve accumulation than projected, with a corresponding rise in reserve money. This feature provides flexibility in accommodating increases in money demand through expanded interventions in the exchange market, thus avoiding below-target inflation.

However, success in attaining monetary and inflation objectives may have been compromised by the simultaneous pursuit of exchange rate stability. In particular, if higher international reserves reflect higher supply of foreign capital—absorbed by the monetary authorities, for example, to avoid appreciation pressures—the increase could be inflationary. In fact, the resulting rise in reserve money (and thereby in commercial bank liquidity) could provide the basis for higher domestic bank credit and thus result in an even larger increase in broad money through the multiplier effect. Changes in reserve money supply can be minimized through offsetting domestic transactions, but such sterilization can be costly. Even countries labeled as independently floating (see Table 3.2)

---

[10]It should be noted that more than one operating target may be employed simultaneously, reflecting multiple policy objectives (see below) as well as uncertainty regarding transmission channels. See, for example, Stone (2003).

[11]As of mid-2004, 26 of the 38 PRGF arrangements incorporated this NDA-NFA framework. Under three programs, a ceiling was set on reserve money instead of central bank NDA (Guinea, Rwanda, and Uganda—of which the latter two are included in the sample of mature stabilizers); Vietnam has a ceiling on NDA of the banking system. For Nicaragua, which maintains a crawling exchange rate peg, and for the member countries of regional monetary unions, neither ceiling applies.

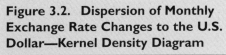

Table 3.2. De Facto Exchange Regimes, 2001

Currency union: Benin, Senegal

Conventional fixed peg to single currency: Bangladesh[1]

Forward-looking crawling band: Honduras

Tightly managed floating: Azerbaijan, Guyana, Mongolia

Other managed floating: Ethiopia, Kyrgyz Republic, Rwanda

Independently floating: Albania, Madagascar, Mozambique, Tanzania, Uganda

Source: Bubula and Ötker-Robe (2002).

[1]Fixed to the U.S. dollar, but with periodic adjustments, until mid-2003, when the currency was floated.

Figure 3.2. Dispersion of Monthly Exchange Rate Changes to the U.S. Dollar—Kernel Density Diagram

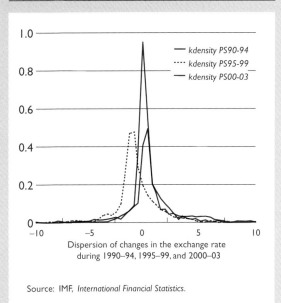

Source: IMF, *International Financial Statistics.*

in practice often intervene to limit exchange rate variability. Moreover, the evidence is strongly suggestive of declining exchange rate flexibility in the mature stabilizers over time. This point is illustrated in Figure 3.2. For the 13 countries in this sample without a hard peg during 1990–94, 1995–99, and 2000–03, the dispersion of the monthly exchange rate changes is more highly concentrated around the mean (0.3 percent) in 2000–03 than earlier periods or relative to other PRGF countries not included in the mature stabilizer sample.[12]

The recent experience of the mature stabilizers shows that the expansion of monetary aggregates has generally been higher than targeted, but without leading to a significant overshooting of inflation targets (Table 3.3).[13] On average, actual broad money growth exceeded program projections by some 4–6 percentage points, about one-third as much as initially envisaged. The average deviation declines as the target approaches (except between $t - 2$ and $t - 1$), which points to increasing accuracy as the projection period shortens (see Appendix I for evidence of improved

program accuracy in consecutive program updates). At the same time, there is little evidence that the higher-than-targeted broad money growth has translated into higher inflation: deviations of inflation from target are not statistically significant, and regression analysis reveals no statistically significant relation between the deviations from the previous years' projections of money growth and inflation, as illustrated by Figure 3.3.[14] It is important to recognize that these findings are fully consistent with the expected positive association between money growth and inflation—which is strongly supported by the data in our sample. Although there was scope to accommodate somewhat higher-than-projected money demand, a further increase in money supply would still have been inflationary.

The evidence that larger-than-programmed monetary growth has not triggered above-target inflation appears limited to the sample of mature stabilizers. Notably, the 2004 review of program design did find statistically significant correlation

[12]In the 20-odd countries with PRGF programs without a hard peg and excluded from the sample, the average monthly change during 2000–03 was 1.8 percent.

[13]Equation (2) in Box 3.2 provides a useful framework for interpreting these data. Rewriting this equation, (projected) inflation can be approximated as a function of the growth rates in broad money (g_M), velocity (g_v), and GDP growth (g_y):

$$g_P = g_M + g_v - g_y,$$

or substituting for broad money growth using the growth rates of reserve money (g_{RM}) and the reserve money multiplier (g_m):

$$g_P = g_{RM} + g_m + g_v - g_y.$$

[14]Deviations from the current-year projections of money growth and inflation also do not exhibit a significant positive correlation. The largest outliers relate to the Mozambique program. Following the floods in 2000, a monetary expansion pushed up broad money growth to 44 percent, after which (year-end) CPI inflation peaked at 22 percent in 2001.

Table 3.3. Monetary Projections and Projection Deviations
(Averages, in percent)

| | \multicolumn{4}{c}{Projection as of[1]} | | | | |
	$t-2$	$t-1$	$t(SR1)$	$t(SR2)$	Outcome
Projected					
Inflation (end-year CPI)	4.1	4.9	6.0	5.9	6.3
Inflation (GDP deflator)	4.3	5.2	6.3	6.1	6.8
Real GDP growth	6.0	5.9	4.9	4.9	5.1
Broad money growth	12.0	12.3	12.2	13.3	17.5
Reserve money growth	...	10.5	9.7	10.3	15.7
NDA contribution[2]	...	−0.6	−6.8	−7.8	−11.5
NFA contribution[2]	...	10.3	16.4	18.2	27.1
Velocity (% change)	...	−0.6	−0.4	−1.6	−4.3
Money multiplier (% change)	...	1.6	2.7	3.1	2.4
No. of observations	29	43	54	54	54
Deviations from projections[3,4]					
Inflation (end-year CPI)	−0.7	−0.5	−0.3	−0.4	
Inflation (GDP deflator)	−1.0	−1.0	−0.5	−0.7	
Real GDP growth	0.2	0.6	−0.2	−0.2	
Broad money growth	4.5**	−5.9***	−5.4***	−4.3***	
Reserve money growth	...	−4.6*	−6.0***	−5.4***	
NDA contribution[2]	...	6.9	5.1	3.7	
NFA contribution[2]	...	−13.1	−11.3**	−8.9*	
NDA contribution[5]	...	−4.1	−6.1	−0.7	
Velocity (% change)	...	4.5***	3.8***	2.7***	
Money multiplier (% change)	...	−1.4	0.2	0.7	

Sources: IMF staff reports and World Economic Outlook database.

[1]The projections are for year t. The projections as of years $t-1$ and $t-2$ are those from the last staff reports in the previous year and the year before that, respectively. The projection as of $t(SR1)$ is from the first staff report in year t, and the one at $t(SR2)$ is from the final staff report in that year. If only one staff report was issued in year t, the last two observations coincide.

[2]NDA (NFA) contribution is defined as the change in central bank NDA (NFA) divided by previous year's reserve money.

[3]Projection deviations are calculated as program values minus outcomes. Because the panel is unbalanced, deviations from the $t-1$ and $t-2$ projections do not correspond to the difference between the average projection for the sample subset and the average outcome for the full sample.

[4]Significance at 10 percent level (*), 5 percent level (**), or 1 percent level (***).

[5]The contribution of the deviation in NDA growth, to the deviation in reserve money growth, transformed to be mapped into (−100, 100),— comparable to the measure in the 2004 evaluation of program design (IMF 2004d, Table 10).

between slippage relative to the one-year-ahead projections in broad money growth and in inflation (IMF, 2004d, Section III.B).[15] That analysis, however, covered all PRGF countries rather than a subset of mature stabilizers.[16] Moreover, the study also

showed that the larger overruns are recorded by high-inflation cases.

The above-target monetary expansion has accommodated a trend decline in velocity. The gradual decline in inflation (Section II) seems to have fostered an increase in broad money demand in real terms (that is, a decrease in velocity)—with lower inflation expectations, the opportunity costs of holding non-interest-bearing financial assets also fall.[17] Financial sector development has likely also contributed to this trend. However, the baseline assumption in most programs has been for velocity to remain largely unchanged (see Figure 3.4), with only a minor average decline. As a result, velocity has on average been 3–5 percent lower than projected

---

[15]The program design review study did not find a significant effect of deviations from projected money growth on inflation for the full sample of PRGF programs, but such effect was found in the subsample of cases in which money growth exceeded the projected level and also on inflation in the following year. By contrast, for the mature stabilizers, no such effect is found when the sample is limited to cases with an overrun in money growth.

[16]A further difference with the current analysis is that the program design review was based on data up to 2000, and thus mainly reflected experience under Enhanced Structural Adjustment Facility (ESAF)-supported programs rather than PRGF-supported programs.

[17]See also IMF (2004f, Box 5).

Figure 3.3. Deviations from Previous-Year Projections for CPI and Broad Money Growth[1]

(In percentage points)

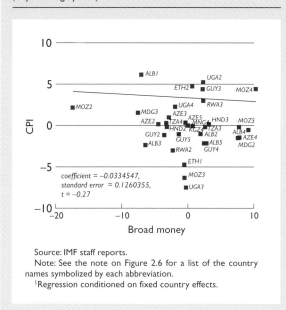

Source: IMF staff reports.

Note: See the note on Figure 2.6 for a list of the country names symbolized by each abbreviation.

[1]Regression conditioned on fixed country effects.

Figure 3.4. Projected and Actual Percentage Change in Velocity

(In percent)

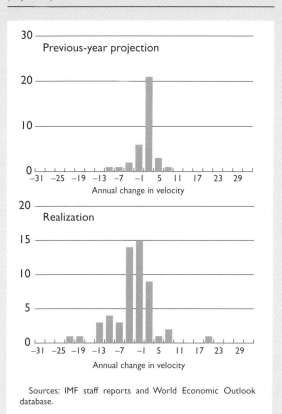

Sources: IMF staff reports and World Economic Outlook database.

(Table 3.3).[18] By contrast, the 2004 program design review found that the null hypothesis of equality of the relationship between money growth and inflation in the program and in reality could not be rejected.[19] Findings concerning average velocity mask the pronounced variation in the changes in this parameter—which have a root mean squared error (RMSE) for velocity growth (in percent) of 7.0 for the final projection.[20] This volatility imparts greater uncertainty to estimates of money demand, complicating the conduct of monetary policy.

The overruns in broad money growth were primarily a reflection of higher-than-projected reserve money growth, the aggregate over which the monetary authorities have most direct control. Program targets for reserve and broad money were exceeded in approximately the same degree (Table 3.3),

---

[18]Further evidence is provided by tests for weak efficiency (Appendix II)—testing if a better projection could be made given a data set that includes just the projection itself—that reject this hypothesis for the projections of money growth and velocity, but not for inflation.

[19]IMF (2004f, Section III.B).

[20]This is compared with an average deviation of 2.7 percentage points. The RMSE is a measure of size of forecasting accuracy, giving the size of the typical deviation, based on a quadratic loss function, and thus weighting large deviations relatively heavily. When the RMSE significantly exceeds the average deviation, there are some deviations that differ significantly from the average.

because the program assumptions for the reserve money multiplier—the parameter that measures the link between the two aggregates—were on average broadly accurate.[21] The deviations in the multiplier from the program assumptions were not statistically significant. Averages, however, mask a great deal of volatility (Figure 3.5).[22]

In turn, higher-than-targeted reserve money growth has mainly reflected larger-than-programmed accumulation of international reserves. As shown in Table 3.3 (upper panel), on average, programs correctly project a decline in central bank NDA and a rise in NFA. However, both changes tend to be even larger than projected, with the NFA overrun exceeding the

---

[21]This is in line with other recent studies (IMF 2004d, Box 3), which have found that the multiplier has remained fairly stable and predictable across all types of IMF-supported programs.

[22]This is reflected in an RMSE of its percentage growth rate of 9.4 for the final staff report, compared with an average deviation of 0.7 percentage point.

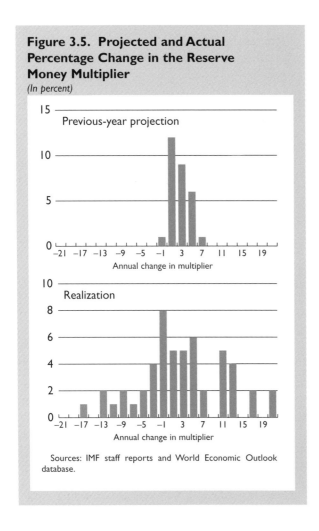

Figure 3.5. Projected and Actual Percentage Change in the Reserve Money Multiplier

(In percent)

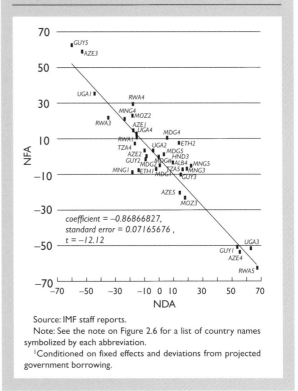

Figure 3.6. Deviations from the Programmed Levels of NDA and NFA[1]

Source: IMF staff reports.
Note: See the note on Figure 2.6 for a list of country names symbolized by each abbreviation.
[1]Conditioned on fixed effects and deviations from projected government borrowing.

Sources: IMF staff reports and World Economic Outlook database.

NDA shortfall, resulting in a faster-than-projected expansion in reserve money.

This additional liquidity expansion is consistent with the architecture of the IMF-supported programs. Conditionality in IMF-supported programs generally requires NDA to be kept below and NFA to be kept above the targets set under the program.[23] Recognizing the uncertainty that attends to estimates of money demand, IMF-supported programs generally do not impose firm limits on the aggregate increase in reserve money. The framework effectively allows for larger-than-programmed monetary expansion to take place as long as it reflects higher reserve accumulation.

Larger-than-programmed monetary and reserves expansion likely also reflects the objective of avoiding appreciation pressures in the face of external inflows. The systematic overruns in NFA growth seem related to the above-mentioned potential tension between reserve money objectives and (de facto) exchange rate targets. Had primacy been given to the money target, greater exchange rate flexibility would have been evident, along with less of a buildup in reserves. More than three-fourths of these NFA overruns have been sterilized through a lower central bank NDA (see Figure 3.6).[24] Thus, monetary authorities have sought to keep foreign inflows from affecting the exchange rate while mitigating their impact on (reserve) money. The relative success of this strategy is illustrated in Figure 3.7: across country episodes, no association between exchange rate stability and overruns in NFA or money growth was apparent.[25] Nonetheless, given the serious costs and limits of

---

[23]Deviations from the projected year-end NDA or NFA level need not indicate that program conditions were missed. First, the deviation may be covered by a program adjuster. Second, generally, only two of the four end-quarter projections serve as performance criteria under the program, whereas the other two merely function as indicative targets.

[24]For a given deviation from the targeted NFA level, most was offset through a divergence in NDA in the opposite direction, with an offset coefficient of about 0.8.

[25]Interpretation is, however, complicated by the endogenous nature of exchange rate stability, which reflects not only the policy orientation but also the incidence of exogenous shocks.

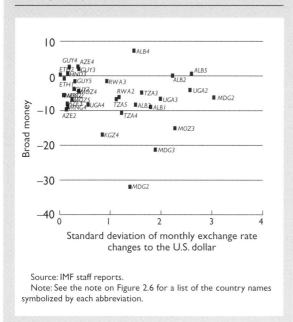

Figure 3.7. Exchange Rate Variability and Deviations from Previous-Year Broad Money Projection

Source: IMF staff reports.
Note: See the note on Figure 2.6 for a list of the country names symbolized by each abbreviation.

appears to provide a useful safety valve, allowing money growth to adjust to unforeseen changes in velocity. However, given the risks to inflation posed by an unwarranted expansion in reserves and money—evident in the larger set of PRGF programs more than in the subsample of mature stabilizers—the use of this channel merits close monitoring. In this context, indicative targets for reserve money growth could provide a useful check. Money growth in excess of the indicative ceiling should prompt further analysis to determine whether monetary policy merely accommodated higher money demand or entailed risk of inflationary pressure.

In the case of a managed floating exchange rate, interventions in the exchange market to resist durable real appreciation pressures may pose risks to the programmed inflation objective. The benefits of a managed float include that it can help absorb real internal and external shocks—which are prevalent in PRGF countries—through nominal exchange rate adjustment. However, the arrangement puts the responsibility for ensuring low and stable inflation firmly on the central bank. Resisting lasting appreciation pressure from such shocks through large-scale—and costly—interventions, building up NFA, and fueling inflation would negate the adjustment mechanism and undermine price stability.[27]

Is Private Sector Credit Being Crowded Out?

Concerns regarding the potential crowding out of private sector credit are an important reason why IMF-supported programs limit domestic financing of the public sector.[28] The desire to foster the growth of credit to the private sector is influenced by findings that financial development, as measured by the volume of intermediated finance, is robustly associated with higher per capita income growth. At the same time, crowding out of credit to the private sector is generally difficult to establish. First, credit markets rarely clear through changes in interest rates alone. Because higher interest rates are likely to attract less creditworthy clients, banks often resort to credit rationing—a behavior not easily captured in the data. Second, financial repression remains prevalent in a number of the mature stabilizers (for example,

sterilization—including the adverse impact of higher real interest rates on private sector growth—for those countries in the mature stabilizer sample with the most heavily managed exchange rates, IMF staff has generally advocated a stronger focus on monetary objectives and a more market-based exchange rate.[26]

These developments in the mature stabilizers point to the potential benefits of some changes in the design of monetary programs. First, there is scope for improving the programming assumptions regarding velocity, which are key to the conduct of monetary policy as well as financial programming. In particular, once inflationary pressures are at bay, monetary projections require a careful assessment of velocity trends and of the need to allow for a (further) decline. With this adjustment, the financial programming framework would continue to be a useful tool for guiding program design, as monetary management remains focused on monetary aggregates rather than interest rates. Second, the standard NDA-NFA framework for monetary policy in IMF-supported programs

[26]This was discussed in the most recent IMF staff reports for Azerbaijan, Ethiopia, Guyana, and Tanzania. This advice is not inconsistent with the evidence on the importance of avoiding overvaluation, as discussed in IMF (2005d). The adverse effects of large-scale intervention and sterilization imply that if overvaluation (and "Dutch disease") is an overriding concern, sharp increases in aid-based spending should be avoided.

[27]See also IMF (2005c).
[28]Similarly, an ambitious target for building up international reserves, or a combination of large-scale intervention and sterilization in response to high aid inflows, can also constrain the room for domestic borrowing and, given government borrowing, for the provision of credit to the private sector. The other important reason for limiting domestic financing is its high cost—particularly relative to the external financing on concessional terms, which is available to most of the mature stabilizers.

Table 3.4. Credit to the Private Sector[1]
(Annual percent growth)

	Program	Actual
Average	19.1	17.7
Median	17.6	15.1
Mode	13.0	20.0
Standard deviation	12.4	24.5
Sample size	40	40

Source: IMF staff estimates.
[1]Credit growth in nominal terms during the first programmed year.

Figure 3.8. Cumulated Growth in Credit and GDP, 1995–2002
(In percent)

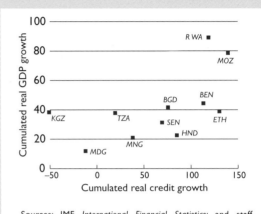

Sources: IMF, *International Financial Statistics*; and staff estimates.
Note: See the note on Figure 2.6 for a list of the country names symbolized by each abbreviation.

Ethiopia), making interest rates sticky. Third, the poor health of the banking sector may inhibit the effectiveness of financial intermediation—limiting the impact of changes in government borrowing on private credit growth. And although there are a few studies (Christensen, 2004; Adam and Bevan, 2004) that find some evidence of crowding out in African countries, in particular, this may capture mainly the cases with severe macroeconomic imbalances. Adam and Bevan (2004) have also flagged the absence of *crowding in* of private sector credit after recourse to domestic financing by the government has been curtailed and broader macroeconomic stability achieved.

Against this backdrop, this section briefly considers, first, the magnitude of private sector credit growth (PSCG) accommodated in IMF-supported programs and, second, the extent to which crowding out, or lack of crowding in, has been problematic.

How Has PSCG Fared in the Mature Stabilizers?

Private sector credit growth in the countries in the sample has expanded at a rapid pace—albeit from a small base and remaining slightly lower than implicitly allowed for in their PRGF-supported programs. On average, during 2000–03, PRGF-supported programs envisaged private sector credit growth on the order of 19 percent—in real terms, about twice the pace of real GDP growth. Actual credit growth was marginally less (just under 18 percent, Table 3.4).[29] More generally, private sector credit growth in the mature stabilizers compares favorably with that in

other low-income countries. The median increase in the ratio of private sector credit to GDP in the sample over the 1995–2003 period was 5 percentage points of GDP, compared with 2½ percentage points in other low-income countries.

However, these averages mask important cross-country variations. Over the somewhat longer horizon of 1995–2003, credit to the nongovernment sector has grown significantly faster than income for most of the mature stabilizers, but particularly so for Bangladesh, Benin, Ethiopia, Honduras, and Senegal (see Figure 3.8). One possible explanation is in the deeper banking systems—the ratio of credit to GDP was about 18 percent in these 5 countries, compared with 11 percent in the other 10 mature stabilizer countries. Also, for some countries (Mozambique, Rwanda, and Tanzania), the association between GDP and credit growth is more linear.[30] However, at least in the case of Rwanda, this likely reflects GDP recovery from extremely low levels more than a positive effect of private credit on real growth.

Crowding Out

There is limited evidence of government recourse to domestic financing crowding out private sector borrowing in the mature stabilizers:

---

[29]This implies an elasticity of PSCG with respect to GDP growth of close to 2 during 2000–03. Over the longer period of 1995–2003, this elasticity was lower (1.5) and below an estimated elasticity of 1.7 for some 146 developed and developing countries over 1995–2003.

[30]In the case of the Kyrgyz Republic, the decline in credit is due to the liquidation of two loss-making state banks; PSCG was positive in real terms between 1997 and 2003. In Madagascar, it reflects poor and highly volatile growth performance.

Figure 3.9. Domestic Debt and Private Sector Credit in Low-Income Countries[1]

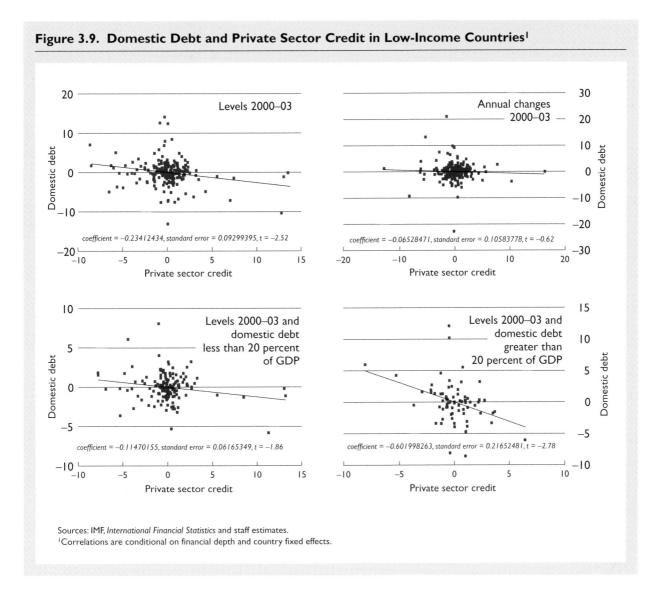

Sources: IMF, *International Financial Statistics* and staff estimates.
[1]Correlations are conditional on financial depth and country fixed effects.

- First, in both the mature stabilizers and the broader grouping of low-income countries, credit to the private sector tends to be lower when levels of domestic debt are higher (Figure 3.9, top left panel). Further, the higher the stock of debt, the more pronounced this negative correlation tends to be (Figure 3.9, lower right panel compared with lower left panel). However, when one looks at annual changes in these variables instead of levels (Figure 3.9, top right panel), the correlation is still negative but no longer statistically significant.

- Second, as noted above, over the somewhat longer period of 1995–2003, credit growth in the mature stabilizers has actually been higher than in other low-income countries, against the backdrop of a similar increase (about 2 percentage points of GDP) in domestic indebtedness in both groups.

- Third, real interest rates (proxied by average treasury bill rates) have remained broadly unchanged in the 15 countries. Beyond this, there is no robust evidence of a negative association between real interest rates and changes in domestic government indebtedness for either the sample or the broader low-income countries grouping. Although, as noted above, crowding out could take place through channels other than interest rates (for example, credit rationing).

These considerations suggest that domestic financing should be relied upon only cautiously, especially where domestic and total debt stocks are high. The absence of convincing evidence notwithstanding, the risk of crowding out should not be discounted too readily—especially given the crucial role of private investment for sustaining growth. Caution in domestic borrowing is also warranted because domestic debt carries higher real interest rates than foreign debt; many projects may have an expected return exceeding the terms of concessional financing, but few projects are likely to have returns exceeding the interest rates on nonconcessional domestic borrowing. For countries that satisfy these conditions, one benchmark to help guide domestic borrowing decisions could be to ensure that annual recourse to such credits is consistent with stabilizing the debt stocks.

IV   Fiscal Policy Issues in PRGF-Supported Programs

This section assesses whether program design in the fiscal area is consistent with the best practices suggested in the literature. It begins with a discussion of the links between fiscal policy and growth, including the channels through which fiscal policy affects economic activity.

Fiscal Stance and Economic Growth

The links between budget deficits and growth go beyond the traditional macroeconomic channels in low-income countries. A number of studies indicate that low levels of the budget deficit and public debt can promote growth.[1] However, the precise channels through which deficits affect growth in low-income countries have received little attention. One study that has specifically examined this topic indicates that budget deficits have only a small effect on growth via the crowding out of investment (Baldacci, Hillman, and Kojo, 2004). The effect of fiscal consolidation on growth through its salutary effects on inflation is also modest. Baldacci, Hillman, and Kojo's study suggests that other factors are at play, including the effect of reductions in expenditure on total factor productivity in countries with poor governance. In light of these findings, this section considers factors that need to be considered in choosing the optimal path for the fiscal balance over the short to medium term in the mature stabilizer sample. A closely related issue is the appropriate measure of the fiscal stance in low-income countries where most of the financing is on concessional terms; this is addressed in Box 4.1 and Appendix III.

The implication of the fiscal stance for debt sustainability is of first-order importance in assessing the optimal path of the fiscal balance. Without sustainability, debt will continue rising to high levels,

hindering growth. Macroeconomic imbalances are also likely to reemerge, with further adverse effects on development.

Given the importance of sustainability, the IMF has recently made efforts to strengthen the framework for assessing debt sustainability. In low-income countries, this has entailed the forward-looking analysis of the evolution of the NPV of public and external debt and the establishment of indicative ceilings for the NPV of public and publicly guaranteed external debt (see IMF, 2004b, 2004e). This framework also stresses the need to take a comprehensive view of debt sustainability that examines not just the evolution of debt ratios, but also debt-service ratios and gross financing needs under a variety of alternative scenarios. It also stresses the importance of assessing whether macroeconomic assumptions underlying baseline scenarios are realistic in light of historical averages. Unfortunately, however, such detailed public sector DSAs for the sampled countries are limited, because systematic preparation of DSAs for low-income countries started only recently. Assessments of debt sustainability in most mature stabilizer countries must therefore be based on more limited data.

Available data suggest that debt sustainability remains a concern in many mature stabilizer countries.[2] Of the 14 countries for which debt data are available on an NPV basis, half had NPV of debt-to-GDP ratios above 40 percent at end-2003 (excluding debt that has since been forgiven under the HIPC Initiative; see Table 4.1). Debt remains especially high in Albania, Ethiopia, Guyana, the Kyrgyz Republic, and Mongolia. Similarly, staff analysis indicates that fewer than half the mature stabilizers have been running primary balances in recent years that would be sustainable under somewhat neutral macroeconomic assumptions (for example, average real GDP growth of 3 percent, constant real exchange rate, and external borrowing

---

[1]Easterly and Rebelo (1993); Easterly, Rodríguez, and Schmidt-Hebbel (1995); Pattillo, Poirson, and Ricci (2002); Clements, Bhattacharya, and Nguyen (2004); Gupta and others (2005); and Adam and Bevan (2005).

[2]Assessments of debt sustainability should take into account multiple indicators and country-specific factors such as the quality of institutions and policies.

Table 4.1. NPV of Public Sector Debt for Selected Poststabilization Countries[1]
(In percent of GDP)

	Fiscal Coverage	2000 Actual	2001 Actual	2002 Actual	2003 Actual	2003 Net of future HIPC relief[2]	2008 Projection	Date of HIPC Completion Point
Albania	General government	...	...	...	58.6	58.6	48.3	Non-HIPC
Bangladesh	Central government	30.0	32.4	34.1	33.5	33.5	31.0	Non-HIPC
Benin	Central government	34.6	36.8	33.4	19.5	19.5	...	Mar. 2003
Ethiopia	General government	...	...	...	61.5	61.5	57.1	Apr. 2004
Guyana	Nonfinancial public sector	144.1	151.5	132.2	104.3	104.3	...	Dec. 2003
Honduras	Nonfinancial public sector	...	...	...	62.9	41.5	...	Mar. 2005
Kyrgyz Republic	General government	...	82.1	86.2	74.5	74.5	...	Non-HIPC
Madagascar	Central government	...	...	...	77.1	42.7	...	Oct. 2004
Mongolia	General government	64.3	61.7	61.9	64.2	64.2	...	Non-HIPC
Mozambique	Central government	31.7	27.1	28.9	25.2	25.2	21.6	Sep. 2001
Rwanda	Central government	...	...	...	67.9	23.6	...	Mar. 2005
Senegal	Central government	55.9	54.2	57.6	45.7	32.6	30.7	Apr. 2004
Tanzania	Central government	...	52.9	26.4	26.4	26.4	...	Nov. 2001
Uganda	Central government	21.8	26.1	30.4	38.5	38.5	34.0	May 2000

Source: IMF staff estimates.

[1]The NPV of public debt is defined here as the sum of the NPV of public and publicly guaranteed external debt plus the nominal value of domestic public debt. Data on domestic public debt are from a Policy Development and Review (PDR) Department database; data on external public- and publicly guaranteed debt are from the HIPC database as of June 2004. External debt data for non-HIPCs are from staff reports. Figures have been updated for countries that have completed a public sector DSA using the new low-income country template or that reached HIPC completion points after June 2004. Data are not available for Azerbaijan.

[2]For comparison purposes, the NPV of public debt is also expressed net of HIPC debt relief for those countries that reached the completion point after the 2003 fiscal year.

with an average grant element of 40 percent; see Appendix IV), although primary balances in a majority of the countries would be sustainable under more optimistic assumptions (for example, real GDP growth of 5 percent). The IMF staff's baseline scenarios project a gradual decline in debt ratios in several cases, but these scenarios sometimes assume real GDP growth that is significantly higher and fiscal policy that is significantly tighter than in the recent past. In some cases, debt is sustainable in the baseline scenario, but not in the event of modest shocks (see Box 4.2 for a discussion of the debt sustainability issue in Ethiopia).

A tighter fiscal stance, higher levels of concessionality in borrowing, or both are therefore required to place public debt on a sustainable path in many countries. In these cases, fiscal policy should target deficits that are sufficiently low and debt management policies should ensure that borrowing terms are sufficiently concessional to avoid debt sustainability problems in the future, including in the event of modest shocks. In many cases, this is likely to require an increase in grant resources (through direct grants, debt relief, or more highly concessional loans) to meet the twin objectives of debt sustain-

ability and providing sufficient funding for spending related to MDGs.

Once countries achieve sustainable deficits at moderate debt levels, they may not benefit from further fiscal consolidation. A number of studies suggest that the deficit-growth nexus is nonlinear. The level at which deficit reduction no longer boosts growth, however, is subject to considerable uncertainty. One recent study (Adam and Bevan, 2005) suggests a breakpoint for the overall deficit (including grants) centered at 1½ percent of GDP, but with wide confidence intervals. Other studies conclude that reducing deficits has no growth payoff for those that have maintained deficits that average less than 2½ percent of GDP (Baldacci, Hillman, and Kojo, 2004; Gupta and others, 2005). In contrast, the average deficit level in the sample countries is about 4½ percent (see Table 2.3).

In countries with clearly sustainable fiscal positions, the productivity of additional outlays should be carefully assessed relative to the costs of financing. In countries with poor governance, the low productivity of outlays may be such that higher spending has a limited effect on growth and social indicators (see also the "Public Expenditure" sub-

---

Box 4.1. Treatment of Concessional Loans in Fiscal Accounts

The appropriate treatment of concessional loans in fiscal accounts has been a subject of lively debate in recent years. Under the accounting rules used by most developing countries, concessional loans are currently recorded in fiscal accounts as a financing item at their face value. Interest payments, at concessional rates, are recorded as expenditure.

Some observers prefer to conceive of a concessional loan as a combination of a nonconcessional loan and a grant. They argue that the grant element of a concessional loan should be treated in fiscal accounts as revenue, analogous to other grants. This would imply that the grant component of the loan is provided upfront, at the time the loan is disbursed. Consistent accounting would require that interest payments on such loans should then be recorded, not at the actual concessional rate, but rather at the higher, nonconcessional rate on the nongrant component of the loan.

These two approaches have different effects on the measured deficit. Under the standard approach, a concessional loan lowers the deficit over the entire lifespan of the loan (relative to a nonconcessional loan) through lower interest payments. In contrast, recording the grant element up front as revenue would lower the deficit immediately (relative to the standard approach). However, subsequent deficits would be larger, reflecting higher interest rates.

The choice between these two approaches would not affect how much spending is sustainable. Under the standard approach, the deficit path that stabilizes the NPV of debt could be identified conditionally on certain financing terms and other macroeconomic assumptions. Under the alternative approach, the measured deficit in the current period might be lower because of the inclusion of the grant element of loans in revenue. However, under this alternative approach, a lower deficit would also be required to stabilize the NPV of debt, because the interest rate on debt would also be higher under this approach. The implications for spending would be the same. The distinction would be that changes in the terms of financing would affect the NPV of the debt-stabilizing deficit under the standard approach, but not under the alternative approach.

The alternative approach is, however, administratively demanding. Given these complexities, it is appropriate to continue the current practice of recording savings from concessional interest rates at the time interest is paid, rather than at the time the loan is contracted. However, deficit targets measured under the standard approach should be evaluated periodically and appropriately adjusted when the terms of financing change.

---

section below). In particular, countries with limited absorptive capacity may also not be in a position to increase spending while ensuring that these outlays are productive (see Box 4.3). The scope for fiscal expansion would also need to take into account fiscal vulnerabilities in the face of exogenous shocks, including those due to the variability of aid. Furthermore, given the rigidity of spending commitments, especially for current outlays, the fiscal risks associated with increases in spending would also need to be assessed. Finally, in countries where debt burdens are more moderate, the pace at which new debt is accumulated needs to be monitored closely.

With inflation broadly under control, fiscal consolidation is not needed to reduce inflationary pressures. This is a result of the limited impact of changes in the fiscal stance on inflation, as well as the uncertain impact of inflation on growth (see Section II). In the same vein, considerations regarding the possible crowding out of the private sector through public sector deficits may also need to play but a small part in determining the appropriate fiscal stance, given the dearth of evidence that deficits have had a large impact on private investment.

At times, PRGF-supported programs have sought to accommodate higher externally financed spending without due regard to debt sustainability considerations. Programs have targeted increases in expenditure in line with higher grants and external financing. Higher budget deficits have also been accommodated in some instances (Section II). At the same time, programs have attempted to promote debt sustainability by limiting nonconcessional external borrowing and domestic financing, even when domestic debt has been at very low levels. However, this combination of policies has not always been sufficient to ensure debt sustainability, as noted above. A heightened focus on debt sustainability (both external and public sector) and the need for more grant financing is thus warranted and should be facilitated by the new DSA framework.

Public Expenditure

In most countries, the government has a central role in providing infrastructure, education, and health services. Thus, the quantity and quality of these services will be critical not only for achieving higher growth, but also for reaching the MDGs. The goals of higher growth and meeting the MDGs are interrelated, because human capital can be a powerful engine of economic growth, including in low-

---

Box 4.2. Public Debt Sustainability: The Case of Ethiopia

IMF staff recently compiled a detailed public and external debt sustainability analysis (DSA) for Ethiopia (IMF, 2004b) using the new DSA templates for low-income countries. Ethiopia thus provides a useful case study for whether program design in such countries is appropriately geared toward achieving debt sustainability.

In the staff's baseline scenario, public sector debt declines gradually. The NPV of public sector debt declines from 55 percent of GDP in 2003 to 52 percent of GDP by 2008 and then to 35 percent of GDP by 2022. Gross financing needs and debt-to-revenue ratios similarly decline.

However, this scenario is based on projected primary deficits and growth rates that are significantly better than historical averages. In the baseline, the primary deficit will be limited to 3 percent of GDP over 2005–10, compared with an average over the past 10 years of 6 percent of GDP, while real GDP will grow at 5¼ percent, well above the 3¾ percent average over the past 10 years.

Under less optimistic assumptions, the NPV of public sector debt will continue to rise. Although the past weak fiscal performance was due in part to the conflict with Eritrea, there is no guarantee that internal or external shocks will not reoccur. In the event that the real average growth rate in the baseline scenario is reduced slightly, to 4¼ percent of GDP, the DSA projects that the NPV of public sector debt would continue rising slowly, to 59 percent of GDP by 2022. If the primary deficit and real GDP growth remain at their historical averages, the DSA projects that the NPV of public sector debt will rise more rapidly, reaching 80 percent of GDP by 2022.

Nonetheless, ratios of debt service to revenue are projected to remain moderate even in less optimistic scenarios, presumably as a result of the long maturity structure of Ethiopia's concessional debt. In the baseline scenario, the ratio of debt service to revenue is expected to remain at about the 2004 level of 6 percent. Under the scenario in which the primary deficit and real GDP growth are at their historical averages, the ratio of debt service to revenue rises continuously but still reaches only 10 percent by 2022. This indicates that, as long as Ethiopia finances its deficit on very concessional terms, near-term debt-service problems are unlikely, although debt service may still become problematic in the long run (20+ years) unless there are significant improvements in growth and fiscal performance.

Such results highlight the critical importance of obtaining financing on sufficiently concessional terms. Given past experience, there is a distinct possibility that such key variables as the primary deficit and real GDP growth will be less favorable than in the baseline scenario, which could result in rising NPV of debt ratios. If the additional financing for deficits is obtained on less concessional terms and with short maturities, debt-service ratios may also rise quickly. These results underscore the need to ensure that minimum levels of concessionality are sufficiently high and deficits sufficiently low so as to make debt sustainability problems unlikely, even in less favorable circumstances.

---

income countries, and growth is vital for poverty reduction.[3]

The average ratio of government spending to GDP in the mature stabilizers is about 26 percent of GDP (the median is 23 percent of GDP), which is relatively low compared to other low- and middle-income countries. During 1999–2003, this ratio was about 29 percent for all low-income countries and 34 percent for middle-income countries. In countries that are members of the Organization for Economic Cooperation and Development, the ratio was about 42 percent. There is also a wide variation among these mature stabilizer countries, with the ratio varying between 14 and 45 percent. The low ratio in most of these countries and the apparent positive relationship between per capita income and government spending suggests that as these countries grow, the share of government spending in GDP is also likely to increase.

Higher spending in sectors related to the MDGs is also expected to raise the ratio of government spending to GDP. Rough estimates of the size of HIV/AIDS disbursements in selected African countries in 2005 reveal that total potential funding could be in excess of 3 percent of GDP in Uganda, about 2 percent in Ethiopia, and more than 1 percent in Mozambique and Tanzania.[4] However, supply bottlenecks (for example, availability of teachers and health sector personnel) will need to be addressed to facilitate the absorption of this external support (see Box 4.2). Other considerations include the sustainability and reliability of aid flows (IMF, 2005c) and the need to avoid excessive levels of debt (see "Fiscal Stance and Economic Growth" in this section). Against this background, the research on the impact of government spending and the composition of government outlays is reviewed here, along with an assessment of lessons for program design.[5]

---

[3]For reviews of this literature, see Krueger and Lindahl (2001) and Baldacci, Hillman, and Kojo (2004).

[4]World Bank (2004c).

[5]The discussion focuses on public spending on infrastructure, education, and health care. For an examination of how public transfers can either retard or promote growth, see Boadway and Keen (2000).

Box 4.3. Absorptive Capacity Constraints and Policies to Ameliorate Them

Absorptive capacity is defined as the amount of spending that can be effectively undertaken by a developing country according to macroeconomic or microeconomic constraints. Absorptive capacity limits are reflected in decreasing returns as spending increases. Macroeconomic constraints are conditions in the recipient country that limit aggregate spending, and microeconomic constraints are specific limitations that can significantly reduce the productivity of spending. The two types of constraints are linked. For example, if aid inflows elicit a strong enough supply response as a result of microeconomic factors, the macroeconomic constraints would be correspondingly reduced. This box focuses on issues related to microeconomic capacity constraints.[1]

At present, the mature stabilizers sample is underexecuting their capital budgets.[2] In this context, scaling up aid and budgeted expenditure could have little effect on capital spending that is executed unless matched by efforts to tackle absorptive capacity constraints.

Absorptive capacity constraints manifest themselves in a number of ways. These include (1) weaknesses in public expenditure management (PEM) systems and low quality of governance;[3] (2) weaknesses in the selection of donor-financed projects resulting in low-productivity projects;[4] (3) weak incentives to adopt good policies and raise the domestic revenue effort to supplement foreign aid;[5] (4) limited skilled labor and

administrative capacity at the sectoral level;[6] (5) high compliance costs of donor conditionality that limit the ability to execute projects;[7] and (6) reliance on project rather than budget support.[8]

Several actions can be taken by both recipient countries and donors to improve absorptive capacity. For recipient countries, the actions are (1) strengthening PEM systems and the quality of governance; (2) improving project selection; (3) reallocating public sector employment to address bottlenecks and improve administrative capacity; and (4) increasing the use of the private sector for service delivery. For donors, the actions include working more closely with recipient countries to integrate donor projects into country poverty reduction strategies, increasing the share of aid as budget support, and improving donor harmonization.

Additional analytical work on absorptive capacity at the country level is also needed. There has been only limited analytical work quantifying absorptive capacity constraints. The additional work could analyze the impact of absorptive capacity constraints on measures of execution and effectiveness of spending at the country level, as well as providing cost estimates of various options to relieve constraints on institutional and human capital and physical infrastructure. Results of these studies could then be incorporated into the countries' PRSPs and provide vital input into medium-term expenditure frameworks.

---

[1]For a discussion of macroeconomic absorptive capacity constraints, see IMF (2005c).

[2]See Section II.

[3]In the 2002 HIPC Initiative tracking assessment, about 90 percent of the countries were found to have inactive or ineffective internal audits. See IMF (2002) for details.

[4]See Hanson and others (2003) and World Bank (2004b).

[5]This manifestation was documented in Gupta and others (2004). However, this effect was not clearly evident in the

mature stabilizer countries in the 1990s: the change in a country's official current transfers was uncorrelated with the change in tax revenue over this period.

[6]See de Renzio (2005) and World Bank (2003, 2004a).

[7]See Radelet and Clemens (2003), Knack and Rahman (2004), and de Renzio (2005).

[8]See World Bank (2004b).

The effect of government spending on growth depends on the macroeconomic context. If macroeconomic stability is lacking, even productive government spending can have an adverse net effect on growth because of its macroeconomic consequences. For the sampled countries, additional spending may be accommodated in some cases without endangering macroeconomic stability, external viability, or public debt sustainability.

Public investment can potentially raise economic growth, although empirical evidence on the impact of public investment on growth remains inconclusive. Data reported in Briceño-Garmendia, Estache, and Shafik (2004) suggest that, of 102 studies that estimate the impact of infrastructure investment on productivity or growth, 53 percent show a significant positive effect, 42 percent show no significant effect,

and 5 percent show a significant negative effect.[6] Still, in a recent survey, Romp and de Haan (2005) suggest that there is more current consensus that public capital furthers economic growth, but the impact is substantially less than what was found in earlier studies, such as that of Aschauer (1989).[7] Recent econometric work suggests that public

---

[6]In multiple-country studies, 40 percent show a positive effect, 50 percent show no significant effect, and 10 percent show a negative effect. In contrast, all 12 single-country developing country studies show a positive effect.

[7]The same authors also caution that "only a few of the enormous bulk of studies on the output effects of infrastructure base their estimates on solid theoretical models," and they suggest that more research is needed on the channels through which infrastructure has an impact on growth.

investment can raise growth in low-income countries and is most productive when governance is good (Tanzi and Davoodi, 2002; Gupta and others, 2005). In this context, more research will also be needed on the channels by which capital expenditure affects growth and how changes in the composition of government spending, including a shift toward capital expenditure, can support growth.

Higher public spending on health and education (both current and capital) can build human capital, but with varying degrees of effectiveness.[8] For example, Baldacci and others (2004) find that an increase in education spending of 1 percent of GDP, holding other factors constant, could increase the net primary enrollment rate by 8 percentage points over a 10-year period. A similar increase in health spending would reduce under-five child mortality by 8 percent over 10 years. Several studies also find that public health care spending may have especially strong effects on the health status of the poor (Gupta, Verhoeven, and Tiongson, 2003; Koenig, Bishai, and Ali Khan, 2001).

However, the composition and efficiency of this social spending are particularly critical. Rates of return for primary and secondary education, for example, exceed those for tertiary education (Psacharopoulos and Patrinos, 2002). Similarly, public health spending that does not substitute for private sector outlays—such as preventive health outlays for immunization that have significant externalities—are likely to have the highest social returns (Hammer, 1993).[9] Primary education and health care expenditures are also more likely to benefit the poor more than other types of spending.[10] At present, however, a large share of spending is allocated to activities that benefit higher-income groups, rather than the poor (Davoodi, Tiongson, and Sawitree, 2003). The mix of spending inputs is also inappropriate in many countries, where a large share of budgetary resources is often used for wages, leaving inadequate funds for nonwage inputs with high productivity, such as medicines and textbooks.[11]

Recent research has emphasized the role of good governance in strengthening the link between social spending and social outcomes.[12] Where institutions are weak, higher spending will have at best a diminished effect on social indicators (Baldacci and others, 2004). In cases where governance is weak, governments are also likely to allocate fewer resources to the social sectors (Mauro, 1998).

The appropriate mix of spending to promote growth and poverty reduction will vary from country to country. Existing research does not provide clear guidance on whether a given country should, at the margin, focus increased spending on health, education, or infrastructure. As such, a country-by-country approach will be needed.[13]

In sum, the literature suggests that countries should focus not only on increasing the level of spending, but also improving the efficiency and targeting of these outlays. Two-thirds of PRGF-supported programs incorporate steps to improve the efficiency of such outlays (Gupta and others, 2002). At the same time, given the large degree of inefficiency in spending, there may be scope for further attention to these issues. The design of reform policies in this area generally falls in the domain of other development partners. To raise the profile of these issues, countries could be encouraged to provide more details on specific social sector reforms in their PRSPs or other country-owned documents.

Programs should continue to emphasize a strengthening of Public Expenditure Management (PEM) systems to improve governance and the effectiveness of spending. Improvements in PEM systems hold promise as a tangible method to strengthen governance. The average PRGF-supported program contains four or five measures to improve PEM systems (Gupta and others, 2002). Given the weaknesses in PEM systems that still prevail in a number of the mature stabilizers, continued integration of PEM reforms into programs remains appropriate.

Tax Policy

This section discusses the appropriate level and structure of tax revenues and the main tax policy issues ahead.

Level and Structure of Taxation

The literature provides little practical guidance on the optimal overall level of taxation. In principle, tax-

---

[8]The results from the literature are far from uniform, however, with some studies showing only a weak or no link between spending and educational outcomes. For a review of this literature, see Baldacci and others (2004) and Kremer (2003).

[9]Empirical evidence for this proposition has, however, been mixed. For example, a case study in Malaysia (World Bank, 1992) found that infant mortality was more strongly affected by increasing immunization than by increasing the number of doctors per capita. In contrast, Gupta, Verhoeven, and Tiongson (2002) find that the share of primary health spending in total health spending has an insignificant effect on aggregate outcomes.

[10]However, some types of tertiary education, such as training of teachers and nurses, may have significant social returns and benefits to the poor.

[11]See, for example, Kremer (2003) and Kremer, Moulin, and Namunyu (2003).

---

[12]See also IMF (2005a).

[13]For a discussion of general frameworks for assessing public expenditure, see Chu and others (1995), Pradhan (1996), and Paternostro, Rajaram, and Tiongson (2004).

ation should be taken to the point at which the marginal social cost of raising an additional $1 equals the marginal social value of the additional expenditure or debt reduction that it finances. In practice, however, the marginal deadweight loss from a tax increase—a key element in this calculation—is subject to considerable empirical uncertainty, and the other elements depend on equity judgments upon which reasonable people may differ. A distinct empirical strand in the literature identifies strong correlations between the overall level of taxation and the level of income per capita, openness, and the importance of the agricultural sector, but these correlations provide little firm guidance for policy, because describing what countries do in general cannot identify what any country in particular should do. For developed countries, however, the evidence suggests that increasing taxes to finance unproductive expenditure adversely affects growth, and higher taxes used for productive expenditure have a positive, albeit mild, effect.[14] The question has received less attention for developing countries, but similar findings have started to emerge.[15]

The tax ratio (tax revenue as a share of GDP) varies widely across the mature stabilizer sample (from 7–10 percent in Bangladesh and Rwanda to 30 percent in Guyana and Mongolia), but has generally increased over the past decade (Table 4.2). On average, it increased from 13.1 percent to 14.9 percent of GDP during the 1990s, and in only two countries—Guyana (where it was initially very high, at 30 percent), and Tanzania—did it fall by more than 1 percentage point. This is a somewhat revenue performance than for the broader set of low-income countries, for which the average rose by only ½ percentage point, to about 15 percent.[16] This result is expected because the sample is a subset that has succeeded in addressing fiscal shortfalls. But the tax ratios they have achieved are not high relative to the wider comparator set, so it is unlikely that many of them have overshot their appropriate levels.

Experience points more clearly to minimum than to maximum levels of taxation, with a ratio of at least 15 percent as a reasonable target for most low-income countries.[17] Few countries have sustained minimally acceptable living standards at tax ratios below 10 percent.[18] At a tax ratio of about 15 per-

cent, most low- to lower-middle-income countries find that increasing revenue requires an expansion of the tax base that is both politically and technically difficult. Achieving a ratio of this order is a reasonable medium-term target for many of these countries. A ratio closer to 20 percent would provide more room for productive expenditures—diminishing returns do not seem to set in quickly—and there is no evidence that it would be intrinsically harmful to growth. However, some countries may reasonably prefer to set somewhat lower tax ratios than this in an attempt to spur economic activity, and the implication is certainly not that all tax rates should be in the 15–20 percent range. A relatively low corporate tax rate, for instance (combined with an appropriate definition of the base) may provide a useful encouragement to private investment.

The composition of tax revenue is also an important concern in policy design. In principle, each tax instrument—the rate of value-added tax (VAT), the extent of investment allowances, and so on—should be taken to the point at which the social cost of raising an additional $1 is the same for all: otherwise, the same revenue could be raised at lower total social cost. Explicit comparisons of this sort can rarely be undertaken, but two important dimensions of choice are of particular interest. The first is the balance between taxes on consumption—including both broad-based commodity taxes (notably the VAT) and excises—and taxes on labor and capital income. At least for developed countries, there is evidence that countries that rely more on consumption taxes tend to save more and grow faster.[19] Against this, personal income taxes provide a better-targeted way of structuring an equitable tax system, although it may well be that spending measures provide an even more effective way of helping the least advantaged. The second is the extent of reliance on customs revenues relative to other sources, there being in principle clear gains to be made in moving from tariffs toward domestic consumption taxes.[20]

The sampled countries have come to rely increasingly on indirect taxes and the VAT in particular. Twelve of the 15 introduced the VAT in the 1990s (Honduras has had one since 1976, Senegal since 1979); Rwanda and Ethiopia introduced the VAT in the early 2000s; only Guyana remains without a VAT (and plans for its adoption are under way). The VAT now accounts on average for nearly 40 percent of tax revenues in the mature stabilizer sample.

---

[14]See Kneller, Bleaney, and Gemmell (1999) and Widmalm (2001).

[15]See Adam and Bevan (2005).

[16]Keen and Simone (2004).

[17]Adam and Bevan (2004) speak of a consensus that the tax ratio for poststabilization countries should be on the order of 15–20 percent.

[18]Of 103 countries examined in Keen and Simone (2004), only 15 had a tax ratio below 10 (and 7 of these were oil producers).

[19]Tanzi and Zee (2000) and Kneller, Bleaney, and Gemmell (1999).

[20]The argument, and its limitations, is spelled out in Keen and Ligthart (2002).

Table 4.2. Evolution of the Revenue Structure of Poststabilization Countries in the 1990s
(In percent of GDP)

	Total Revenue	Nontax Revenue	Tax Revenue							
				Direct taxes			Indirect taxes			
			Total	Total	Personal	Corporate	Total	VAT[1]	Excises	Customs
2000–01[2]										
Albania	22.4	3.3	19.1	6.6	1.0	1.6	10.9	6.9	1.6	2.3
Azerbaijan	21.4	6.8	14.6	6.6	1.9	2.4	7.3	4.4	1.3	1.6
Bangladesh	8.5	1.5	7.0	1.1	...	...	5.5	3.5	0.1	1.8
Benin	16.4	2.0	14.4	3.7	1.4	1.8	10.7	6.0	0.4	3.6
Ethiopia	22.4	9.4	13.0	4.7	1.3	3.1	8.2		0.7	3.2
Guyana	29.8	2.6	27.2	11.5	4.6	5.5	13.7		...	3.7
Honduras	18.0	1.7	16.3	3.7	...	...	12.6	5.6	4.6	2.4
Kyrgyz Republic	19.5	4.1	15.4	6.0	1.2	1.1	7.8	5.2	1.9	0.4
Madagascar	10.8	0.4	10.4	2.3	0.9	1.0	8.0	4.4	0.5	2.5
Mongolia	36.6	9.0	27.6	10.3	1.7	4.3	15.2	8.5	4.4	2.3
Mozambique	13.3	1.4	11.9	2.0	1.3	0.7	9.6	5.1	2.4	2.2
Rwanda	19.0	9.4	9.6	2.9	1.1	1.7	6.6		2.3	1.8
Senegal	17.8	0.8	17.0	4.0	1.8	1.5	13.1	7.2	0.3	4.5
Tanzania	11.0	1.2	9.8	2.8	1.1	0.9	6.1	3.4	1.6	1.2
Uganda	10.3	0.7	9.6	2.0	...	...	7.6	3.2	3.2	1.2
Average	**18.5**	**3.6**	**14.9**	**4.7**	**1.6**	**2.1**	**9.5**	**5.3**	**1.8**	**2.3**
Early 1990s[3]										
Albania	21.4	5.7	15.7	5.5	...	2.7	9.1		2.8	2.6
Azerbaijan	20.0	8.6	11.4	7.8	1.2	4.0	3.6	1.9	1.0	0.7
Bangladesh	8.7	1.9	6.8	1.2	...	...	5.1	2.8	0.2	2.1
Benin	11.6	2.1	9.5	3.0	1.0	1.1	6.5	2.3	0.5	3.3
Ethiopia	15.6	6.0	9.6	3.1	1.0	1.9	6.5		0.6	1.9
Guyana	33.5	2.2	31.3	11.4	...	...	14.2		...	4.4
Honduras	16.6	1.1	15.5	4.5	...	...	10.8	2.9	3.4	4.6
Kyrgyz Republic	21.9	8.1	13.9	5.8	1.7	3.8	6.5	4.3	1.4	0.4
Madagascar	8.1	0.5	7.6	1.5	0.5	0.8	6.1		0.6	4.6
Mongolia	32.3	5.3	27.1	15.9	...	...	10.6		...	3.1
Mozambique	12.8	1.8	11.0	2.1	0.8	1.3	8.5		2.0	3.2
Rwanda	11.4	4.8	6.6	1.8	0.6	0.7	4.8		1.6	2.1
Senegal	15.1	1.9	13.3	3.4	1.8	1.0	9.9	4.2	0.3	4.5
Tanzania	12.5	1.4	11.1	3.1	0.5	0.8	7.2		2.1	1.6
Uganda	6.8	0.5	6.3	1.0	...	...	5.0		0.6	2.9
Average	**16.6**	**3.5**	**13.1**	**4.7**	**1.0**	**1.8**	**7.6**	**3.1**	**1.3**	**2.8**

Sources: IMF, *World Economic Outlook*, Statistical Annexes (various issues); IMF staff calculations.

[1]VAT includes revenues collected by customs and inland revenue departments. Totals for direct and indirect taxes may not add because of unavailability of data for the subcategories.

[2]Average of two years for all countries and 1999 for Guyana.

[3]Depending on data availability, the average represents two consecutive years between 1990 and 1994.

With some exceptions, these countries have also reduced their reliance on trade taxes. On average—Azerbaijan and Ethiopia are exceptions—these reductions accounted for revenues equivalent to 2.8 percent of GDP in the early 1990s but 2.3 percent at the turn of the century, a modest but worthwhile structural improvement. It is largely by introducing or improving the VAT that these countries have recovered lost trade tax revenues. In Bangladesh, for example, trade tax revenues fell by about 0.3 percent of GDP while revenue from the VAT increased by 0.7 percent. This experience runs counter to the emerging evidence that low-income countries, in general, have not succeeded in recovering lost trade tax revenues.[21] The success of the countries in doing so is important, not least for the example it provides to others.

---

[21]Khattry and Rao (2002) and Keen and Baunsgaard (2004).

Table 4.3. Selected VAT and Corporate Income Tax (CIT) Indicators[1]

		VAT					CIT			
		Rates (%)			C-efficiency ratio (%)		Top marginal rate (%)		CIT to GDP (%)	
	Introduction	Introduction	2003	Other rates	Early 1990s[1]	2000–01[2]	Early 1990s[1]	2003	Early 1990s[1]	2000–01[2]
Albania	July 1996	12.5	20.0		0.34	0.39	30.0	25.0	2.7	1.6
Azerbaijan	Jan. 1992	28.0	18.0		0.13	0.29	45.0	25.0	4.0	2.4
Bangladesh	July 1991	15.0	15.0		0.22	0.29	40.0	30.0	...	...
Benin	May 1991	18.0	18.0		0.29	0.35	48.0	38.0	1.1	1.8
Ethiopia	Jan. 2003	15.0	15.0				50.0	30.0	1.9	3.1
Guyana							55.0	45.0	...	5.5
Honduras	Jan. 1976	3.0	12.0	15.0	0.48	0.46	40.3	25.0	...	...
Kyrgyz Republic	Jan. 1992	28.0	20.0		0.23	0.31	30.0	20.0	3.8	1.1
Madagascar	Sep. 1994	20.0	20.0		0.16	0.29	35.0	35.0	0.8	1.0
Mongolia	July 1998	10.0	15.0		0.70	0.72	40.0	40.0	...	4.3
Mozambique	Jun. 1999	17.0	17.0		0.36	0.36	45.0	32.0	1.3	0.7
Rwanda	Jan. 2001	15.0	18.0				50.0	40.0	0.7	1.7
Senegal	Mar. 1979	20.0	17.0	7.0	0.36	0.60	35.0	35.0	1.0	1.5
Tanzania	July 1998	20.0	20.0		0.17	0.18	50.0	30.0	0.8	0.9
Uganda	July 1996	17.0	17.0		0.21	0.22	40.0	30.0	...	...
Average		**17.0**	**17.3**	**11.0**	**0.30**	**0.37**	**42.2**	**32.0**	**1.8**	**2.1**

Sources: IMF, *World Economic Outlook*; Statistical Appendix (various issues); IMF, Technical Assistance Reports (various issues); KPMG Worldwide Corporate Tax Rates Survey (various issues).

[1]Depending on data availability, the average represents two consecutive years between 1990 and 1994.

[2]Average of two years for all countries and 1999 for Guyana.

Current and Future Tax Policy Issues

The most prominent tax policy issues that need to be addressed for the mature stabilizer countries in the coming years are likely to be as follows:

- ***Strengthening the VAT.*** This is not a matter of increasing rates of the VAT. These are not low by international standards, averaging over 17 percent and with only Honduras now having a standard rate below 15 percent (Table 4.3). Further increases would likely put significant pressure on the wider system by increasing the attractions of noncompliance. The issue is rather to expand the base of the VAT, primarily by reducing exemptions and improving compliance. Gains from this source can be seen in Table 4.3. The C-efficiency is the ratio of VAT revenues to the product of the standard VAT rate and total private consumption. If all consumption were subject to the VAT, C-efficiency would be unity.[22] That is rarely the case even in developed countries, but a ratio closer to 40 than to 30 percent should be within the sights of most sampled countries. C-efficiency has increased in this sample, but there is still scope for significant improvement in some countries. In Bangladesh, for example, increasing C-efficiency to 40 percent would increase the tax ratio by nearly 1 percentage point.

- ***Reducing reliance on trade tax revenues.*** At an average of 16 percent of total tax revenue—and about one-fourth in some—trade taxes remain an important source of revenue. Some degree of trade liberalization may be possible without reducing trade tax revenues further (for example, by eliminating exemptions or by reducing protective tariffs set above revenue-maximizing levels). Although no summary measure can fully describe potentially complex tariff systems and the range of potential reforms, it is notable that all of these countries have collected tariff rates below the 20 percent estimated to be revenue maximizing by Ebrill, Stotsky, and Gropp (1999).[23] With trade tax revenues already declining in most of these countries, continued trade liberalization will intensify the need to improve domestic tax systems. This will often involve strengthening the indirect tax system, including the VAT (reducing exemptions and rate differentiation, for instance). To avoid transitional

[22]Ebrill and others (2001) discuss the limitations of C-efficiency as a summary measure for the assessment of a VAT.

[23]The collected tariff rate—the ratio of tariff revenue to import value—averages about 9 percent, with a range from 1.2 (the Kyrgyz Republic) to 18.3 percent (Benin).

revenue losses, such measures need to be carefully sequenced with those of trade liberalization.

- *Dealing with pressures on corporate tax revenue.* Several of the mature stabilizers have seen a noticeable reduction in their revenue from corporate taxation over the last decade (for example, 1 percentage point in Albania and 1½ points in Azerbaijan (Table 4.2)). Statutory rates of corporate tax have fallen considerably (Table 4.3), from 42.2 percent, on average, to 32 percent. In most of these countries,[24] the loss of revenue has been smaller than the rate reduction alone would imply, suggesting that—again unlike the broader set of all low-income countries—these reductions were accompanied by either a significant supply response or some tightening of tax exemptions. Nevertheless, it seems likely that corporate tax revenues will continue to come under pressure: corporate tax rates continue to fall around the world, and the current rates in the mature stabilizer

---

[24]The exceptions are Albania and the Kyrgyz Republic, where the starting point of the early 1990s reflects the early days of their transition from the strong reliance on corporate taxes under the pretransition tax regimes. Keen and Simone (2004) document a reduction in corporate tax revenues in the wider set of low-income countries, though the underlying data are poor and the role of cyclical factors remains unexplored.

sample are high relative to, for example, some European Union (EU) accession countries. Mitigating this pressure requires avoiding excessive exemptions, such as tax holidays and direct tax breaks for exporters, that not only seem to do little to attract investment but also erode revenue both directly and by creating avoidance opportunities. The most effective way for countries to avoid giving excessive exemptions may be by entering regional agreements, not least because regional trade integration sharpens internal competition for FDI (as with Tanzania within the East African Community). Experience in the EU suggests that issues of corporate tax coordination are best addressed early in the integration process.

Improving tax administration is as important as improving tax design. Strengthening audit capacity, constructing organizational structures that provide appropriate incentives for information exchange, and fair tax enforcement are all critical to the expansion of the tax base, which is key to improving revenue mobilization and reducing the distortions and inequities of their current tax systems. But the potential impact of administrative improvement alone should not be overstated, especially in the short term. The links between design and administration are also key: where compliance and governance are poor, simplicity of design is critical for good administrative performance.

V Conclusions

In sum, macroeconomic outcomes in the low-income countries reviewed in this paper have been robust in recent years, with inflation reduced to single digits, the highest per capita income growth rates for many years, and improved public finances. But notwithstanding these improvements, the foregoing discussion highlights several areas where adjustments to the design of IMF-supported programs could be considered.

First, the economic growth rates that have been registered to date must be sustained; indeed, still higher rates of growth are necessary for stronger inroads in poverty reduction consistent with the MDGs. The modest increase in investment levels in the sample of mature stabilizer countries in recent years is encouraging. But whether higher growth rates can be achieved remains an open question, which depends much more on further changes to economic and political institutions.[1]

Second, external viability and fiscal sustainability remain elusive in most of the mature stabilizers. Some two-thirds of the countries in the sample either already have high external debt burdens that make them susceptible to a heightened risk of debt distress or are maintaining current account deficits that will soon put them in this situation. For this set of countries, the stance of fiscal policy clearly needs to heed debt sustainability considerations. Higher grant resources (either through direct grants or more highly concessional loans) are required to meet the twin objectives of debt sustainability and providing sufficient funding for spending related to the MDGs. In the other one-third of the mature stabilizers, though, there would seem to be somewhat more scope for additional poverty-reducing spending—subject to absorptive capacity constraints being overcome. Further, where debt burdens are more moderate, the pace at which countries accumulate new debt will need to be monitored carefully to avoid the reemergence of debt problems.

Third, improving the quality of public spending as well as public expenditure management systems will be a major challenge in the coming years. Mature stabilizers have been underexecuting their capital budgets in recent years. For example, planned increases in public investment under PRGF-supported programs in the sampled countries have generally failed to materialize. In this context, scaling up aid is unlikely to be productive unless it is also matched by efforts to tackle absorptive capacity constraints.

Finally, the broad objective of monetary policy in PRGF-supported programs should continue to be keeping inflation in the single-digit range. There is evidence from the mature stabilizer sample that with inflationary pressures receding, money demand has increased markedly. This increase in money demand needs to be more systematically accommodated in the design of monetary programs. Where double-digit inflation has resurfaced, it has generally been associated with supply shocks. Given the prevalence of such shocks in low-income countries, IMF-supported programs could consider either targeting a measure of core inflation (where this is practicable) or a target range for inflation (with the midpoint of this range being used for operational purposes).

[1]See IMF (2005b).

Appendix I   The Accuracy of Consecutive Updates of Monetary Projections

As more information becomes available over time, the monetary projections in consecutive program revisions should show increasing accuracy. This expectation is supported by Table 3.3 in the main text, which shows a decreasing mean deviation of the outcomes from the consecutive projections. However, the mean does not provide a full picture. The correlation of successive projections with the outcomes provides additional insight.

For each of the key monetary variables in the panel of 13 countries with observations from 1999 to 2003, Table A1.1 shows the correlation coefficients between the projected percentage changes in the consecutive program updates and the realizations.[1] This statistical procedure follows that used by Atoian and others (2004). To allow for comparison across a balanced panel (given that often projections for broad money and, especially, reserve money are not available), the table includes three lines for each variable. The first (second) line reflects only those

---
[1]Consistent with the section on financial programming, this analysis excludes Benin and Senegal in view of their membership in the CFA franc zone.

Table A1.1. Accuracy of Program Updates
(Correlation coefficients between projections and outcomes)

	No. of observations	Projection at Time[1]			
		$t-2$	$t-1$	$t(SR1)$	$t(SR2)$
Inflation (end-year CPI)	26	0.29	0.29	0.47	0.47
	42		0.30	0.50	0.56
	52			0.43	0.47
Inflation (GDP deflator)	29	0.29	0.35	0.57	0.57
	43		0.35	0.72	0.71
	54			0.60	0.60
Real GDP growth	29	0.48	0.69	0.88	0.89
	43		0.49	0.86	0.88
	54			0.86	0.87
Broad money growth	17	0.61	0.69	0.68	0.82
	32		0.53	0.59	0.80
	53			0.45	0.54
Reserve money growth	10	−0.06	−0.19	0.82	0.76
	29		0.03	0.55	0.57
	54			0.46	0.51
Velocity (% change)	15	0.44	0.38	0.52	0.70
	35		0.00	0.22	0.47
	54			0.39	0.44
Money multiplier (% change)	10	0.27	0.00	0.88	0.72
	29		0.04	0.42	0.49
	54			0.26	0.34

Sources: IMF staff reports and World Economic Outlook database.
[1]The year the projections are for is t. The projections as of year $t-1$ and $t-2$ are those from the last staff reports in the previous year and the year before that, respectively. The projection as of $t(SR1)$ is from the first staff report in year t, and the one at $t(SR2)$ is from the final staff report in that year. If one staff report was issued in year t, the last two observations coincide.

cases in which a projection was included in the final IMF staff report for the country circulated two years (one year) before the year in question, referred to as the $t-2$ ($t-1$) staff report; the third line is based on all cases and relates only to the projections presented in the first—$t(SR1)$—and the last—$t(SR2)$—staff report during the target year.

The results indicate that the accuracy of the projections indeed improves as the time horizon shortens: in almost all cases, the correlation coefficient is higher for projections closer to the realization. The correlation coefficients for reserve money (and the money multiplier), however, are lower for $SR2$ than for $SR1$ for the small subset of cases in which observations were already presented two years in advance.

A second test of projection accuracy, suggested by Musso and Phillips (2001), considers the predictive value of the projections relative to a forecast based on a random walk model (that is, assuming the same percentage change as observed in the previous year). The comparison of the two forecasts is made using Theil's U-statistic (which equals the ratio of the RMSE of the projection to the RMSE of the alternative forecast based on the "no change" scenario). A lower U-statistic implies greater relative accuracy of the program projection; a value of 1 would indicate that the program forecast is no more accurate than the random walk alternative.

The results presented in Table A1.2 show that, in all cases, the program projections had smaller errors

Table A1.2. Test of the Accuracy of Program Projections (Theil's U-Statistic)[1]

| | Projection at Time[2] | |
	$t(SR1)$	$t(SR2)$
Inflation (end-year CPI)	0.78	0.76
Inflation (GDP deflator)	0.74	0.75
Real GDP growth	0.39	0.39
Broad money growth	0.83	0.75
Reserve money growth	0.67	0.64
Velocity (% change)	0.84	0.77
Money multiplier (% change)	0.64	0.62

Source: IMF staff reports and World Economic Outlook database.

[1]The ratio of the RMSE of the actual projections to the RMSE based on a "no change" forecast.

[2]The projection as of $t(SR1)$ is from the first staff report in year t, and the one at $t(SR2)$ is from the final staff report in that year. If only one staff report was issued in year t, the last two observations coincide.

than the random walk alternative. In line with the results in the previous table, the later projections with a shorter horizon had smaller deviations.[2]

[2]The previous year's rate of change could not be observed at time $t-2$ or at $t-1$; thus a comparison of the random walk projection with the program projections made at these earlier stages would not be meaningful.

Appendix II   The Efficiency of Monetary Projections

A standard test of projection efficiency is based on a regression of the actual change on a constant term and the program projection (Musso and Phillips, 2001). A projection is deemed weakly efficient if given an information set that consists of only the historical projection, no systematic projection error can be identified (that is, if the constant does not deviate significantly from zero, and the slope does not deviate from one). The results are shown in Table A2.1 for the projections made in the previous year—$t-1$—and in the current year—$t(SR1)$ and

$t(SR2)$. The asterisks (*) in the body of the table indicate the cases in which the hypothesis of efficiency can be rejected.

The results corroborate the findings presented in the main text based on a comparison of the mean deviations between projections and outcomes: the hypothesis of weak efficiency is rejected for the projections of money growth and velocity, but not for inflation. The higher R^2 for projections made at a later stage support the finding reported in Appendix I of increasing projection accuracy.

Table A2.1. Test of the Weak Efficiency of Program Projections

Regression results: $X^A = b_0 + b_1 * X^P$	b^1	$b_1{}^1$	R^2	No. of Observations
Projections at time $(t-1)^2$				
Inflation (end-year CPI)	0.67	1.00	0.12	41
Inflation (GDP deflator)	2.55	0.70	0.11	43
Real GDP growth	−1.98	1.23	0.24	43
Broad money growth	2.41	1.28	0.28	33
Reserve money growth	13.60*	0.14	0.00	29
Velocity (% change)	−5.14***	−0.01***	0.00	35
Money multiplier (% change)	2.65	0.23	0.00	29
Projections at time $t(SR1)^2$				
Inflation (end-year CPI)	1.23	0.84	0.17	52
Inflation (GDP deflator)	0.78	0.95	0.35	54
Real GDP growth	−0.14	1.06	0.75	54
Broad money growth	6.82**	0.88	0.21	54
Reserve money growth	6.83***	0.92	0.21	54
Velocity (% change)	−4.05***	0.65*	0.15	54
Money multiplier (% change)	1.16	0.48**	0.07	54
Projections at time $t(SR2)^2$				
Inflation (end-year CPI)	0.41	1.06	0.21	52
Inflation (GDP deflator)	1.02	0.95	0.35	54
Real GDP growth	−0.16	1.07	0.75	54
Broad money growth	6.86***	0.81	0.29	54
Reserve money growth	6.90***	0.85	0.26	54
Velocity (% change)	−3.38***	0.59	0.19	54
Money multiplier (% change)	0.63	0.58*	0.11	54

Sources: IMF staff reports and World Economic Outlook database.

[1]Indicating that the null hypotheses of $b_0 = 0$ and $b_1 = 1$ can be rejected at the 90 percent (*), 95 percent (**), or 99 percent (***) confidence level.

[2]The projections as of year $t-1$ are those from the last staff report in the previous year. The projections as of $t(SR1)$ and $t(SR2)$ are from the first and the last staff reports in the year the projections are for.

Appendix III   Measuring the Fiscal Stance and Accounting Issues

The coverage of fiscal statistics varies across countries, as do measures of the fiscal stance. This issue has taken on heightened importance in recent years—it has been argued that alternative measures of the deficit (for example, the current balance) suggest greater scope for expanding public spending than has hitherto been recognized.[1] This appendix reviews best practices in the measurement of the fiscal stance.

The appropriate fiscal stance should be assessed by use of multiple indicators. A single fiscal measure is unlikely to determine whether the fiscal stance is sustainable and appropriate in the context of a country's macroeconomic circumstances. At a minimum, it is appropriate to measure the overall fiscal balance before and after grants and a breakdown of financing into domestic and foreign sources. In some cases, presentations may vary in light of differing institutional arrangements (for example, West African Economic and Monetary Union countries). Regardless of presentation, programs should continue to monitor a range of indicators of the fiscal stance. Key indicators should be tailored to each country's circumstances.[2]

If public debt is at high levels, measures of both external and total public indebtedness should be closely monitored. In this regard, ratios of the NPV of external public debt to exports and the NPV of total public debt to GDP and revenue are useful summary variables of total indebtedness.[3] Ratios of debt service to revenue and gross financing needs to GDP can also indicate whether the path of debt payments is sufficiently smooth to avoid liquidity problems.[4]

Similarly, program design should focus on targeting flow variables that have the most direct impact on debt sustainability. These could include the minimum level of concessionality and the overall deficit.[5] Both of these indicators, however, have limitations: minimum levels of conditionality do not necessarily restrict the total accumulation of new debt, and overall deficit targets do not incorporate the differing effects that concessional and nonconcessional borrowing have on NPV ratios. For these reasons, the new DSA framework for low-income countries also suggests the use of indicative ceilings on NPV ratios (IMF, 2004a). Primary balances, non-oil balances, and arrears may also be useful indicators, depending on country circumstances.

If crowding out or monetary financing of the deficit is a concern, it may be useful to focus on the level of domestic financing or net credit to the government. In cases where external debt is high and growing, however, an exclusive focus on domestic credit would be inadequate.

To ensure comprehensive measurement of the fiscal stance and debt sustainability, fiscal data covered in programs should ideally extend to the general government and noncommercial, nonfinancial public corporations. This approach seeks to strike the appropriate balance between adequately covering fiscal activities and avoiding inappropriate constraints on the investments of commercially run public enterprises (IMF, 2004g). In practice, however, data limitations necessitate a much more narrow coverage. In Africa, for example, less than 20 percent of fiscal statistics monitored by the IMF cover the nonfinancial public sector.[6] In countries where significant fiscal activities are being undertaken outside the area of coverage, PRGF-supported programs should seek to broaden the institutional coverage of the fiscal sector accounts.

---

[1]For a review of these arguments, see IMF (2004g).

[2]This discussion focuses on program design, rather than on fiscal conditionality per se, which is beyond the scope of this paper. Such an assessment would need to take into account, among other things, the timeliness and quality of data and the authorities' ability to control the variables in question.

[3]Separate monitoring of NPV-based indicators is also important because changes in the overall deficit do not accurately reflect changes in government net worth as a result of the grant element of concessional borrowing.

[4]The path of these variables under multiple scenarios can usefully be examined in the context of the DSA.

---

[5]For further discussion of these measures, see IMF (2004e).

[6]Figures are based on the assessment of country documents in IMF (2004c).

Appendix IV   NPV of Debt-Stabilizing Primary Balances

Acommonly used statistic in the debt sustainability literature is the debt-stabilizing primary balance. Following Buiter (1985), the debt-stabilizing primary balance (as a share of GDP), p^* can be expressed as

$$p^* = (r - g)d, \tag{1}$$

where r is the real interest rate on debt, g is the real GDP growth rate, and d is nominal debt as a share of GDP.[1] Incorporating exchange rate effects on debt denominated in foreign currency, equation (1) can be reformulated as

$$p^* = (r + se - g)d, \tag{2}$$

where s is the share of debt held in foreign currency and e is the rate of real exchange rate depreciation. The real interest rate in this expression should be defined as the weighted average of the domestic and foreign real interest rates, where the domestic real interest rate is the nominal interest rate minus inflation and the foreign real interest rate is the nominal interest rate on foreign currency debt minus *foreign* inflation.

Following Baldacci and Fletcher (2004), an analogous expression for the primary balance that stabilizes the NPV of debt would be

$$p^* + f = (z + se - g)n, \tag{3}$$

where z is the real discount rate, n is the NPV of debt, and f is the grant element of new concessional financing (the difference between the nominal value of new financing and the NPV of new financing) as a share of GDP. Intuitively, equation (3) is the same as equation (2), except that the real discount rate, rather than the actual real interest rate, affects the evolution of the NPV of debt and the grant element of new financing is an important factor in determining the debt-stabilizing primary balance. In effect, the grant element of loans is treated as revenue in equation (3) to derive the augmented primary balance, $(p^* + f)$.

The DSA template for low-income countries defines the NPV of total debt in these countries as the NPV of external debt plus the nominal value of domestic debt. In this case, the debt-stabilizing primary balance would be

$$p^* + f = (sz + (1 - s)r^d + se - g)n, \tag{4}$$

where r^d is the real domestic interest rate. If r^d is the same as the foreign real discount rate, then equation (4) collapses back to equation (3).

What does equation (4) imply about the sustainability of the sample of mature stabilizers? Assuming a nominal dollar discount rate of 5 percent and an average U.S. inflation rate over the next 10 years of 2 percent, the real discount rate (z) would be 3 percent. If real domestic interest rates and medium-run growth in the sample countries are assumed to be 3 percent and the real exchange rate appreciation is assumed to be zero, then the augmented primary balance that stabilizes the NPV of debt is zero, irrespective of the level of debt:

$$p^* + f = (0.03 + 0 - 0.03)n = 0. \tag{5}$$

Equation (5) can then be used to examine whether fiscal policy in these countries has been consistent with the objective of debt sustainability.

Unfortunately, data on the actual grant element of new borrowing are not readily available. Using data on net external financing, the grant element of new borrowing can be estimated by assuming that gross external borrowing is 1.25 times net external borrowing and the average grant element is 40 percent of gross borrowing.

These assumptions yield the average debt-stabilizing augmented primary balances for the countries in the sample over the years 2000 to 2003 (Table A4.1). Of the 15 countries, only 6 ran augmented primary surpluses, implying that their fiscal positions were sustainable under the growth and financing assumptions above. In contrast, the majority of countries ran augmented primary deficits and therefore unsustainable policies. However, all but two countries were within 2 percent of GDP of the debt-stabilizing augmented primary balance.

---

[1]Note that equation (1) could also be written using the nominal interest and growth rates (because the inflation elements of both variables would cancel each other out) or in terms of nominal debt and primary balances (by multiplying both sides of the equation by nominal GDP).

Table A4.1. Average Augmented Primary Balance, 2000–2003

Country	Percent of GDP
Albania	−0.8
Azerbaijan	0.6
Bangladesh	−0.3
Benin	−0.3
Ethiopia	−2.2
Guyana	2.7
Honduras	0.9
Kyrgyz Republic	−1.5
Madagascar	−1.1
Mongolia	−1.2
Mozambique	−2.5
Rwanda	−0.4
Senegal	1.1
Tanzania	0.5
Uganda	0.1

Sources: IMF, World Economic Outlook database and staff estimates.

These estimates are, however, sensitive to the assumptions made:

- For example, if these countries grew at 5 percent rather than 3 percent, then a country with an NPV of debt of 50 percent of GDP could run an augmented primary deficit of 1 percent of GDP and still stabilize its debt at the 50 percent level. In this case, 10 of the 15 countries would have been running sustainable policies. Conversely, a growth rate of only 1 percent would require an augmented primary *surplus* of 1 percent of GDP.
- Similarly, if the real exchange depreciated by 2 percent a year, then a country with 75 percent of the debt in foreign currency would need to run an augmented primary surplus of 0.75 percent of GDP to stabilize the NPV of debt at the 50 percent level. Conversely, a constant real appreciation of 2 percent a year would allow an augmented primary deficit of 0.75 percent of GDP.
- Also, the assumption of a common grant element of 40 percent may be quite high for some countries. For example, Guyana's high augmented primary surplus in Table A4.1 is due to high external borrowing, which implies a high effective grant element. In reality, however, the grant element in Guyana may have been much lower, which would mean that the high augmented primary surplus may be misleading.
- The effect of changes in the discount rate is, however, less straightforward. A higher discount rate would affect three variables in equation (4)—the discount rate itself, the NPV of debt, and the grant element of new borrowing. An increase in the discount rate itself would tend to increase the debt-stabilizing primary balance, but would also tend to lower the NPV of existing debt and increase the grant element of new borrowing, both of which would tend to decrease the debt-stabilizing primary balance. The net effect would depend on the structure of the debt.

Some additional caveats should also be borne in mind:

- The fiscal outturns for 2000–03 may not reflect more recent developments. For example, whereas these estimates indicate that Guyana ran a comfortable fiscal policy, they do not reflect the recent large deterioration in Guyana's fiscal position.
- Second, the calculations above assume that countries continue to receive the current level of grants. If the grant to GDP ratio declines, then a corresponding reduction in spending, increase in revenues, or both is needed.
- Third, these calculations do not take account of extrabudgetary activities that increase debt but not deficits.

Therefore, a more detailed, country-specific analysis would be required before any firm conclusions could be reached on the sustainability of any particular country's fiscal policy.

Nevertheless, these calculations may still provide a useful general picture of the *average* fiscal positions across these countries. The picture that emerges is that many of these countries still do not have sustainable fiscal positions, but they are not far away. An improvement in the augmented primary fiscal balance by 1–2 percent of GDP through additional effective grants (either through outright grants or higher grant elements of concessional loans) could result in sustainable fiscal positions for almost all countries in the sample.

References

Adam, Christopher S., and David L. Bevan, 2004, "Fiscal Policy Design in Low-Income Countries," in *Fiscal Policy for Development*, ed. by T. Addison and A. Roe (New York: Palgrave Macmillan).

―――, 2005, "Fiscal Deficits and Growth in Developing Countries," *Journal of Public Economics,* Vol. 89, No. 4, pp. 571–97.

Aschauer, David A., 1989, "Is Public Expenditure Productive?" *Journal of Monetary Economics,* Vol. 23, No. 2, pp. 177–200.

Atoian, Rouben, Patrick Conway, Marcelo Selowski, and Tsidi Tsikata, 2004, "Macroeconomic Adjustment in IMF-Supported Programs: Projections and Reality," IEO Background Paper No. BP/04/2 (Washington: International Monetary Fund).

Baldacci, Emanuele, Benedict Clements, Sanjeev Gupta, and Qiang Cui, 2004, "Social Spending, Human Capital, and Growth in Developing Countries: Implications for Achieving the MDGs," IMF Working Paper 04/217 (Washington: International Monetary Fund).

Baldacci, Emanuele, and Kevin Fletcher, 2004, "A Framework for Fiscal Debt Sustainability Analysis in Low-Income Countries," in *Helping Countries Develop: The Role of Fiscal Policy*, ed. by Sanjeev Gupta, Benedict Clements, and Gabriela Inchauste (Washington: International Monetary Fund).

Baldacci, Emanuele, Ayre L. Hillman, and Naoko Kojo, 2004, "Growth, Governance, and Fiscal Policy Transmission Channels in Low-Income Countries," *European Journal of Political Economy*, Vol. 20, No. 3, pp. 517–49. Also published as Chapter 4 in *Helping Countries Develop: The Role of Fiscal Policy*, ed. by Sanjeev Gupta, Benedict Clements, and Gabriela Inchauste (Washington: International Monetary Fund).

Barro, Robert J., 1996, "Inflation and Economic Growth," *Federal Reserve Bank of St. Louis Review*, Vol. 78, No. 3, pp. 153–69.

Boadway, Robin, and Michael Keen, 2000, "Redistribution," in *Handbook of Income Distribution*, Vol. 1, ed. by A.B. Atkinson and F. Bourguignon (Amsterdam: Elsevier North-Holland).

Briceño-Garmendia, Cecilia, Antonio Estache, and Nemat Shafik, 2004, "Infrastructure Services in Developing Countries: Access, Quality, Costs, and Policy Reform," Policy Research Working Paper 3468 (Washington: World Bank).

Bruno, Michael, and William Easterly, 1998, "Inflation Crises and Long-Run Growth," *Journal of Monetary Economics*, Vol. 41 (February), pp. 3–26.

Bubula, Andrea, and Inci Ötker-Robe, 2002, "The Evolution of Exchange Rate Regimes Since 1990: Evidence from De Facto Policies," IMF Working Paper 02/155 (Washington: International Monetary Fund).

Buiter, Willem, 1985, "Guide to Public Sector Debt and Deficits," *Economic Policy: A European Forum*, Vol. 1 (November), pp. 13–79.

Bulíř, Ales, 2001, "Income Inequality: Does Inflation Matter?" *Staff Papers*, International Monetary Fund, Vol. 48, No. 1, pp. 139–59.

Burdekin, Richard C.K., Arthur T. Denzau, Manfred W. Keil, Thitithep Sitthiyot, and Thomas D. Willett, 2000, "When Does Inflation Hurt Economic Growth? Different Nonlinearities for Different Economies," Claremont Colleges Working Paper in Economics 2000-22 (Claremont, California. Claremont McKenna College).

Christensen, Jakob, 2004, "Domestic Debt in Sub-Saharan Africa," IMF Working Paper 04/46 (Washington: International Monetary Fund).

Chu, Ke-young, Sanjeev Gupta, Benedict Clements, Daniel Hewitt, Sergio Lugaresi, Jerald Schiff, Ludger Schuknecht, and Gerd Schwartz, 1995, "Unproductive Public Expenditures: A Pragmatic Approach to Policy Analysis," IMF Pamphlet Series No. 48 (Washington: International Monetary Fund).

Clements, Benedict, Rina Bhattacharya, and Tuan Quoc Nguyen, 2004, "External Debt, Public Investment and Growth in Low-Income Countries," in *Helping Countries Develop: The Role of Fiscal Policy*, ed. by Sanjeev Gupta, Benedict Clements, and Gabriela Inchauste (Washington: International Monetary Fund).

Davoodi, Hamid, Erwin H. Tiongson, and Sawitree S. Asawanuchit, 2003, "How Useful Are Benefit Incidence Analyses of Public Education and Health Spending?" IMF Working Paper 03/227 (Washington: International Monetary Fund).

de Renzio, Paolo, 2005, "Can More Aid Be Spent in Africa?" *Opinions* (London: Overseas Development Institute). Available via the Internet: www.odi.org.uk/publications/opinions.

Easterly, William, 2004, "National Policies for Economic Growth: A Reappraisal," NYU Development Research Working Paper No. 1. Available via the Internet: http://papers.ssrn.com/sol3/papers.cfm?abstract_id=507402.

―――, and Ross Levine, 2003, "Tropics, Germs, and Crops: The Role of Endowments in Economic Development," *Journal of Monetary Economics*, Vol. 50, No. 1, pp. 3–47.

Easterly, William, and Sergio Rebelo, 1993, "Fiscal Policy and Economic Growth: An Empirical Investigation," *Journal of Monetary Economics*, Vol. 32, No. 3, pp. 417–58.

Easterly, William, Carlos A. Rodríguez, and Klaus Schmidt-Hebbel, 1995, *Public Sector Deficits and Macroeconomic Performance* (New York: Oxford University Press).

Ebrill, Liam, Michael Keen, Jean-Paul Bodin, and Victoria Summers, 2001, *The Modern VAT* (Washington: International Monetary Fund).

Ebrill, Liam, Janet Stotsky, and Reint Gropp, 1999, "Revenue Implications of Trade Liberalization," IMF Occasional Paper No. 180 (Washington: International Monetary Fund).

Fischer, Stanley, 1993, "The Role of Macroeconomic Factors in Growth," *Journal of Monetary Economics*, Vol. 32, No. 3, pp. 45–66.

———, and William Easterly, 2001, "Inflation and the Poor," *Journal of Money, Credit and Banking*, Vol. 33, No. 2, pp. 160–78.

Ghosh, Atish, and Steven Phillips, 1998, "Warning: Inflation May Be Harmful to Your Growth," *Staff Papers*, International Monetary Fund, Vol. 45 (November), pp. 672–710.

Gupta, Sanjeev, Benedict Clements, Emanuele Baldacci, and Carlos Mulas-Granados, 2005, "Fiscal Policy, Expenditure Composition, and Growth in Low-Income Countries," *Journal of International Money and Finance* (April), pp. 441–63. Also published as Chapter 2 in *Helping Countries Develop: The Role of Fiscal Policy*, ed. by Sanjeev Gupta, Benedict Clements, and Gabriela Inchauste (Washington: International Monetary Fund).

Gupta, Sanjeev, Benedict Clements, Alexander Pivovarsky, and Erwing Tiongson, 2004, "Foreign Aid and Revenue Response: Does the Composition of Aid Matter?" in *Helping Countries Develop: The Role of Fiscal Policy*, ed. by Sanjeev Gupta, Benedict Clements, and Gabriela Inchauste (Washington: International Monetary Fund).

Gupta, Sanjeev, Mark Plant, Benedict Clements, Thomas Dorsey, Emanuele Baldacci, Gabriela Inchauste, Shamsuddin Tareq, and Nita Thacker, 2002, "Is the PRGF Living Up to Expectations? An Assessment of Program Design," IMF Occasional Paper No. 216 (Washington: International Monetary Fund).

Gupta, Sanjeev, Marijn Verhoeven, and Erwin R. Tiongson, 2002, "The Effectiveness of Government Spending on Education and Health Care in Developing and Transition Economies," *European Journal of Political Economy*, Vol. 18, No. 4, pp. 717–37. Also published as Chapter 8 in *Helping Countries Develop: The Role of Fiscal Policy*, ed. by Sanjeev Gupta, Benedict Clements, and Gabriela Inchauste (Washington: International Monetary Fund).

———, 2003, "Public Spending on Health Care and the Poor," *Health Economics*, Vol. 12, No. 8, pp. 685–96. Also published as Chapter 9 in *Helping Countries Develop: The Role of Fiscal Policy*, ed. by Sanjeev Gupta, Benedict Clements, and Gabriela Inchauste (Washington: International Monetary Fund).

Gylfason, Thorvaldur, and Tryggvi T. Herbertsson, 2001, "Does Inflation Matter for Growth?" *Japan and the World Economy*, Vol. 13, No. 4, pp. 405–28.

Hammer, Jeffrey, 1993, "Prices and Protocols in Public Health Care," Policy Research Working Paper 1131 (Washington: World Bank).

Hanson, Kara, M. Kent Ranson, Valeria Oliveira-Cruz, and Anne Mills, 2003, "Expanding Access to Priority Health Interventions: A Framework for Understanding the Constraints to Scaling Up," *Journal of International Development*, Vol. 15 (special issue), No. 1, pp. 1–14.

International Monetary Fund, 2002, "Actions to Strengthen the Tracking of Poverty-Reducing Public Spending in Heavily Indebted Poor Countries (HIPC)" (Washington, March 22). Available via the Internet:http://www.imf.org/External/np/hipc/2002/track/032202.htm.

———, 2004a, "Debt Sustainability in Low-Income Countries—Further Considerations on an Operational Framework and Policy Implications" (Washington, September 10). Available via the Internet: http://www.imf.org/external/np/pdr/sustain/2004/091004. htm.

———, 2004b, "Debt Sustainability in Low-Income Countries—Proposal for an Operational Framework and Policy Implications" (Washington, March 12). Available via the Internet: http://www.imf.org/external/np/fad/2004/pifp/eng/index.htm.

———, 2004c, "Fund-Supported Programs: Objectives and Outcomes" (Washington, November 24). Available via the Internet: http://www.imf.org/external/np/pdr/2004/eng/object.pdf.

———, 2004d, "Macroeconomic and Structural Policies in Fund-Supported Programs: Review of Experience" (Washington, November 24). Available via the Internet: http://www.imf.org/external/np/pdr/2004/eng/macro.htm.

———, 2004e, "Operational Framework for Debt Sustainability Analysis in Low-Income Countries Implications for Fund Program Design" (Washington, September 13). Available via the Internet: http://www.imf.org/external/np/par/sustain/2004/191304.pdf.

———, 2004f, "Policy Formulation, Analytical Frameworks and Program Design" (Washington, November 24). Available via the Internet: http://www.imf.org/external/np/pdr/2004/eng/policy.htm.

———, 2004g, "Public Investment and Fiscal Policy" (Washington, March 12). Available via the Internet: http://www.imf.org/external/np/fad/2004/pifp/eng/index.htm.

———, 2005a, "Can PRGF Policy Levers Improve Institutions and Lead to Sustained Growth?" (Washington, August 8). Available via the Internet: http://www.imf.org/external/np/pp/eng/2005/080805L.htm.

———, 2005b, "The Federal Democratic Republic of Ethiopia—Debt Sustainability Analysis," IMF Country Report 05/27 (Washington, January).

———, 2005c, "The Macroeconomics of Managing Aid Inflows: Experiences of Low-Income Countries and Policy Implications" (Washington, August 8). Available via the Internet: http://www.imf.org/external/np/pp/eng/2005/080805a.htm.

———, 2005d, "Operational Framework for Debt Sustainability Assessments in Low-Income Countries—Further Considerations" (Washington, March 28). Available via the Internet: http://www.imf.org/external/np/pp/eng/2005/032805.pdf.

Independent Evaluation Office (IEO), 2004, *Report on the Evaluation of Poverty Reduction Strategy Papers (PRSPs) and the Poverty Reduction and Growth Facility (PRGF)* (Washington: International Monetary Fund).

Keen, Michael, and Thomas Baunsgaard, 2004, "Tax Revenue and (or?) Trade Liberalization" (Washington: International Monetary Fund).

Keen, Michael, and Jenny Ligthart, 2002, "Coordinating Tariff Reductions and Domestic Tax Reform," *Journal of International Economics*, Vol. 56, No. 2, pp. 407–25.

Keen, Michael, and Alejandro Simone, 2004, "Tax Policy in Developing Countries: Some Lessons from the 1990s and Some Challenges Ahead," in *Helping Countries Develop: The Role of the Fiscal Policy*, ed. by Sanjeev Gupta, Benedict Clements, and Gabriela Inchauste (Washington: International Monetary Fund).

Khan, Mohsin S., and Abdelhak S. Senhadji, 2001, "Threshold Effects in the Relation between Inflation and Growth, *Staff Papers*, International Monetary Fund, Vol. 48, No. 1, pp. 1–21.

Khattry, Barsha, and J. Mohan Rao, 2002, "Fiscal Faux Pas? An Analysis of the Revenue Implications of Trade Liberalization," *World Development*, Vol. 30, No. 8, pp. 1431–44.

Knack, Stephen, and Aminur Rahman, 2004, "Donor Fragmentation and Bureaucratic Quality in Aid Recipients," Policy Research Working Paper 3186 (Washington: World Bank).

Kneller, Richard, Michael F. Bleaney, and Norman Gemmell, 1999, "Fiscal Policy and Growth: Evidence from OECD Countries," *Journal of Public Economics*, Vol. 74, No. 2, pp. 171–90.

Kochhar, Kalpana, and Sharmini Coorey, 1999, "Economic Growth: What Has Been Achieved So Far and How?" in *Economic Adjustment and Reform in Low-Income Countries*, ed. by Hugh Bredenkamp and Susan Schadler (Washington: International Monetary Fund).

Koenig, Michael, David Bishai, and Mehrab Ali Khan, 2001, "Health Interventions and Health Equity: The Example of Measles Vaccination in Bangladesh," *Population and Development Review*, Vol. 27, No. 2, pp. 283–302.

Kremer, Michael, 2003, "Randomized Evaluations of Educational Programs in Developing Countries: Some Lessons," *American Economic Review, Papers and Proceedings,* Vol. 3 (May), pp. 102–06.

———, Sylvie Moulin, and Robert Namunyu, 2003, "Decentralization: A Cautionary Tale" (unpublished; Cambridge, Massachusetts: Harvard University).

Krueger, Alan, and Mikael Lindahl, 2001, "Education for Growth: Why and for Whom?" *Journal of Economic Literature*, Vol. 39 (December), pp. 1101–36.

Li, Hongyi, and Heng-fu Zou, 2002, "Inflation, Growth, and Income Distribution: A Cross-Country Study," *Annals of Economics and Finance,* Vol. 3, No. 1, pp. 85–101.

Mauro, Paolo, 1998, "Corruption and the Composition of Government Expenditure," *Journal of Public Economics*, Vol. 69, No. 2, pp. 263–79.

Musso, Alberto, and Steven Phillips, 2001, "Comparing Projections and Outcomes of IMF-Supported Programs," IMF Working Paper 01/45 (Washington: International Monetary Fund).

Paternostro, Stefano, Anand Rajaram, and Erwin R. Tiongson, 2004, "How Does the Composition of Public Spending Matter?" (unpublished; Washington: World Bank).

Pattillo, Catherine, Helene Poirson, and Luca Ricci, 2002, "External Debt and Growth," IMF Working Paper 02/69 (Washington: International Monetary Fund).

Phillips, Steven, 1999, "Inflation: The Case for a More Resolute Approach," in *Economic Adjustment and Reform in Low-Income Countries*, ed. by Hugh Bredenkamp and Susan Schadler (Washington: International Monetary Fund).

Pradhan, Sanjay, 1996, "Evaluating Public Spending: A Framework for Public Expenditure Reviews," Discussion Paper 323 (Washington: World Bank).

Psacharopoulos, George, and Harry Patrinos, 2002, "Returns to Investment in Education: A Further Update," Policy Research Working Paper 2881 (Washington: World Bank).

Radelet, Steven, and Michael Clemens, 2003, "The Millennium Challenge Account: How Much Is Too Much, How Long Is Long Enough?" Working Paper 23 (Washington: Center for Global Development).

Romp, Ward, and Jakob de Haan, 2005, "Public Capital and Economic Growth: A Critical Survey," *EIB Papers* Vol. 10, No. 1, pp. 40–70.

Sarel, Michael, 1996, "Nonlinear Effects of Inflation on Economic Growth," *Staff Papers*, International Monetary Fund, Vol. 43 (March), pp. 199–215.

Stone, Mark, 2003, "Inflation Targeting Lite," IMF Working Paper 03/12 (Washington: International Monetary Fund).

Tanzi, Vito, and Hamid Davoodi, 2002, "Corruption, Public Investment, and Growth," in *Governance, Corruption, and Economic Performance*, ed. by Sanjeev Gupta and George Abed (Washington: International Monetary Fund).

Tanzi, Vito, and Howell Zee, 2000, "Taxation and the Household Saving Rate: Evidence from OECD Countries," *Quarterly Review/Banca Nazionale del Lavoro*, Vol. 53, No. 212, pp. 31–43.

Temple, Jonathan, 2000, "Inflation and Growth: Stories Short and Tall," *Journal of Economic Surveys*, Vol. 14, No. 4, pp. 395–426.

Widmalm, Frida, 2001, "Tax Structure and Growth: Are Some Taxes Better than Others?" *Public Choice*, Vol. 107, Nos. 3–4, pp. 199–219.

World Bank, 1992, "Malaysia: Fiscal Reform for Stable Growth," Report 10120-MA, East Asia and Pacific Region (Washington).

———, 2001, *Poverty Reduction Strategy Sourcebook: A Resource to Assist Countries in Developing Poverty Reduction Strategies* (Washington).

———, 2003, "Supporting Sound Policies with Adequate and Appropriate Financing," paper presented to the Development Committee, Washington, September 22.

———, 2004a, "Aid Effectiveness and Financing Modalities," paper presented to the Development Committee, Washington, October 2.

———, 2004b, *Global Monitoring Report 2004, Policies and Actions for Achieving the Millennium Development Goals and Related Outcomes*, Vol. 1 (Washington).

———, 2004c, "Strengthening Capacity for Dialogue between Ministries of Finance and Health in Africa: Scaling Up the HIV/AIDS Response" (unpublished; Washington).

World Bank and International Monetary Fund, 2005, *Global Monitoring Report 2005—Millennium Development Goals: From Consensus to Momentum* (Washington: World Bank).

Recent Occasional Papers of the International Monetary Fund

250. Designing Monetary and Fiscal Policy in Low-Income Countries, by Abebe Aemro Selassie, Benedict Clements, Shamsuddin Tareq, Jan Kees Martijn, and Gabriel Di Bella. 2006.

249. Official Foreign Exchange Intervention, by Shogo Ishi, Jorge Iván Canales-Kriljenko, Roberto Guimarães, and Cem Karacadag. 2006.

248. Labor Market Performance in Transition: The Experience of Central and Eastern European Countries, by Jerald Schiff, Philippe Egoumé-Bossogo, Miho Ihara, Tetsuya Konuki, and Kornélia Krajnyák. 2006.

247. Rebuilding Fiscal Institutions in Post-Conflict Countries, by Sanjeev Gupta, Shamsuddin Tareq, Benedict Clements, Alex Segura-Ubiergo, Rina Bhattacharya, and Todd Mattina. 2005.

246. Experience with Large Fiscal Adjustments, by George C. Tsibouris, Mark A. Horton, Mark J. Flanagan, and Wojciech S. Maliszewski. 2005.

245. Budget System Reform in Emerging Economies: The Challenges and the Reform Agenda, by Jack Diamond. 2005.

244. Monetary Policy Implementation at Different Stages of Market Development, by a staff team led by Bernard J. Laurens. 2005.

243. Central America: Global Integration and Regional Cooperation, edited by Markus Rodlauer and Alfred Schipke. 2005.

242. Turkey at the Crossroads: From Crisis Resolution to EU Accession, by a staff team led by Reza Moghadam. 2005.

241. The Design of IMF-Supported Programs, by Atish Ghosh, Charis Christofides, Jun Kim, Laura Papi, Uma Ramakrishnan, Alun Thomas, and Juan Zalduendo. 2005.

240. Debt-Related Vulnerabilities and Financial Crises: An Application of the Balance Sheet Approach to Emerging Market Countries, by Christoph Rosenberg, Ioannis Halikias, Brett House, Christian Keller, Jens Nystedt, Alexander Pitt, and Brad Setser. 2005.

239. GEM: A New International Macroeconomic Model, by Tamim Bayoumi, with assistance from Douglas Laxton, Hamid Faruqee, Benjamin Hunt, Philippe Karam, Jaewoo Lee, Alessandro Rebucci, and Ivan Tchakarov. 2004.

238. Stabilization and Reforms in Latin America: A Macroeconomic Perspective on the Experience Since the Early 1990s, by Anoop Singh, Agnès Belaisch, Charles Collyns, Paula De Masi, Reva Krieger, Guy Meredith, and Robert Rennhack. 2005.

237. Sovereign Debt Structure for Crisis Prevention, by Eduardo Borensztein, Marcos Chamon, Olivier Jeanne, Paolo Mauro, and Jeromin Zettelmeyer. 2004.

236. Lessons from the Crisis in Argentina, by Christina Daseking, Atish R. Ghosh, Alun Thomas, and Timothy Lane. 2004.

235. A New Look at Exchange Rate Volatility and Trade Flows, by Peter B. Clark, Natalia Tamirisa, and Shang-Jin Wei, with Azim Sadikov and Li Zeng. 2004.

234. Adopting the Euro in Central Europe: Challenges of the Next Step in European Integration, by Susan M. Schadler, Paulo F. Drummond, Louis Kuijs, Zuzana Murgasova, and Rachel N. van Elkan. 2004.

233. Germany's Three-Pillar Banking System: Cross-Country Perspectives in Europe, by Allan Brunner, Jörg Decressin, Daniel Hardy, and Beata Kudela. 2004.

232. China's Growth and Integration into the World Economy: Prospects and Challenges, edited by Eswar Prasad. 2004.

231. Chile: Policies and Institutions Underpinning Stability and Growth, by Eliot Kalter, Steven Phillips, Marco A. Espinosa-Vega, Rodolfo Luzio, Mauricio Villafuerte, and Manmohan Singh. 2004.

230. Financial Stability in Dollarized Countries, by Anne-Marie Gulde, David Hoelscher, Alain Ize, David Marston, and Gianni De Nicoló. 2004.

229. Evolution and Performance of Exchange Rate Regimes, by Kenneth S. Rogoff, Aasim M. Husain, Ashoka Mody, Robin Brooks, and Nienke Oomes. 2004.

228. Capital Markets and Financial Intermediation in The Baltics, by Alfred Schipke, Christian Beddies, Susan M. George, and Niamh Sheridan. 2004.

227. U.S. Fiscal Policies and Priorities for Long-Run Sustainability, edited by Martin Mühleisen and Christopher Towe 2004.

226. Hong Kong SAR: Meeting the Challenges of Integration with the Mainland, edited by Eswar Prasad, with contributions from Jorge Chan-Lau, Dora Iakova, William Lee, Hong Liang, Ida Liu, Papa N'Diaye, and Tao Wang. 2004.

225. Rules-Based Fiscal Policy in France, Germany, Italy, and Spain, by Teresa Dában, Enrica Detragiache, Gabriel di Bella, Gian Maria Milesi-Ferretti, and Steven Symansky. 2003.

224. Managing Systemic Banking Crises, by a staff team led by David S. Hoelscher and Marc Quintyn. 2003.

223. Monetary Union Among Member Countries of the Gulf Cooperation Council, by a staff team led by Ugo Fasano. 2003.

222. Informal Funds Transfer Systems: An Analysis of the Informal Hawala System, by Mohammed El Qorchi, Samuel Munzele Maimbo, and John F. Wilson. 2003.

221. Deflation: Determinants, Risks, and Policy Options, by Manmohan S. Kumar. 2003.

220. Effects of Financial Globalization on Developing Countries: Some Empirical Evidence, by Eswar S. Prasad, Kenneth Rogoff, Shang-Jin Wei, and Ayhan Kose. 2003.

219. Economic Policy in a Highly Dollarized Economy: The Case of Cambodia, by Mario de Zamaroczy and Sopanha Sa. 2003.

218. Fiscal Vulnerability and Financial Crises in Emerging Market Economies, by Richard Hemming, Michael Kell, and Axel Schimmelpfennig. 2003.

217. Managing Financial Crises: Recent Experience and Lessons for Latin America, edited by Charles Collyns and G. Russell Kincaid. 2003.

216. Is the PRGF Living Up to Expectations?—An Assessment of Program Design, by Sanjeev Gupta, Mark Plant, Benedict Clements, Thomas Dorsey, Emanuele Baldacci, Gabriela Inchauste, Shamsuddin Tareq, and Nita Thacker. 2002.

215. Improving Large Taxpayers' Compliance: A Review of Country Experience, by Katherine Baer. 2002.

214. Advanced Country Experiences with Capital Account Liberalization, by Age Bakker and Bryan Chapple. 2002.

213. The Baltic Countries: Medium-Term Fiscal Issues Related to EU and NATO Accession, by Johannes Mueller, Christian Beddies, Robert Burgess, Vitali Kramarenko, and Joannes Mongardini. 2002.

212. Financial Soundness Indicators: Analytical Aspects and Country Practices, by V. Sundararajan, Charles Enoch, Armida San José, Paul Hilbers, Russell Krueger, Marina Moretti, and Graham Slack. 2002.

211. Capital Account Liberalization and Financial Sector Stability, by a staff team led by Shogo Ishii and Karl Habermeier. 2002.

210. IMF-Supported Programs in Capital Account Crises, by Atish Ghosh, Timothy Lane, Marianne Schulze-Ghattas, Aleš Bulíř, Javier Hamann, and Alex Mourmouras. 2002.

209. Methodology for Current Account and Exchange Rate Assessments, by Peter Isard, Hamid Faruqee, G. Russell Kincaid, and Martin Fetherston. 2001.

208. Yemen in the 1990s: From Unification to Economic Reform, by Klaus Enders, Sherwyn Williams, Nada Choueiri, Yuri Sobolev, and Jan Walliser. 2001.

207. Malaysia: From Crisis to Recovery, by Kanitta Meesook, Il Houng Lee, Olin Liu, Yougesh Khatri, Natalia Tamirisa, Michael Moore, and Mark H. Krysl. 2001.

206. The Dominican Republic: Stabilization, Structural Reform, and Economic Growth, by a staff team led by Philip Young comprising Alessandro Giustiniani, Werner C. Keller, and Randa E. Sab and others. 2001.

205. Stabilization and Savings Funds for Nonrenewable Resources, by Jeffrey Davis, Rolando Ossowski, James Daniel, and Steven Barnett. 2001.

Note: For information on the titles and availability of Occasional Papers not listed, please consult the IMF's *Publications Catalog* or contact IMF Publication Services.